A I A I G A S A

Quentin S. Crisp was born in 1972, in North Devon, U.K. He studied Japanese at Durham University and graduated in 2000. He has had fiction published by Tartarus Press, PS Publishing, Eibonvale Press and others. He currently resides in Bexleyheath, and is editor for Chômu Press.

SNUGGLY BOOKS

QUENTIN S. CRISP

AIAIGASA

With illustrations by
Beehive Crick

THIS IS A SNUGGLY BOOK

ISBN: 978-1-943813-65-0

Contents

AIAIGASA

相合い傘

Poems

歌

2nd November

—

Small, plastic hoops seen
Through the windows of trains—tired
Geometries I've
Known since ninety-seven. This,
Not cyber-zen, is Japan.

二

On the train, across
From us, a couple tease each
Other. He grabs or
Pushes her head. Even such
Horse-play is self-conscious, forced.

三

An izakaya,
Our first night. Gentle rain. As
We leave, the cook who
Served us brings an umbrella,
Tartan, large enough for two.

3rd November

—

The old tales mention
Names of plants as if they were
Gateways to other
Worlds. These days the gateways are
All closed; the plants are just plants.

二

Blocks rise from the moat
Surrounding the castle. Weeds
Mass over concave
Angles. A double image
Forms—this world and that of dream.

三

On a bench among
Trees in the park surrounding
The castle, a man
Smokes a cigarette, unshaved
On a Monday afternoon.

四

The electronic
Chimes and voices from public
Buildings, transport, lifts—
Japan's a wind-up music
Box, circled by crows.

五

Night. I go for a
Piss and hear running water.
No friend like the moon,
This stream that runs by the house,
Just time, silence, lonely death.

六

Midnight. You found me
In the laundry room. I think
We'd both been crying.
I hope you'll always find me
Like that—never a stranger.

七

Sliding door shuts. Sounds
This clear enforce silence. You
Stare at bedding, at
Matting, afraid. A sense of
Unhome that almost becomes home.

4th November

—

At Katsura we
Change trains. You observe there are
Stylish people here.
The train's deep red and brown: a
Sepia, steam-era mood.

二

Tiny, almost too
Small, the red leaves of the vine,
Almost too perfect,
On the stone lantern in this
Silent-film actor's garden.

三

A garden made for
Film sets. On the path I kissed
You, but didn't say
How I felt like an actor—
An actor of silent films.

5th November

—

The rolling rumble
Of the bathroom door was deep
In memory and
Now is heard again. It means
Nothing except life goes on.

二

Just dark. We find a
Knick-knack café empty but
For us. The moment
We see the lady wants to
Close, she apologises.

三

A special evening
Viewing. In the courtyard, to
A collective sigh,
Blue lights fade up. They belong
Here—the Blue Lotus Temple.

四

Steps lead to a shrine.
Lit from below, the bamboo
Grove shines blue-white with
Otherworldly light, each leaf
Still, exact, as if cut out.

五

Last month I promised
You roasted chestnuts. By chance
Here they are, sold on
Philosopher's Walk in brown
Paper bags—yama kuri.

6th November

一

At the altar where
People kneel, the Buddha who
Looks back. All living
Things will fall through the bottom
Of bottomlessness. He waits.

二

In the building of
Shôren-in Temple, I see
Two sides of Japan:
Clean, sweeping line of roof and
Fungus of calligraphy.

三

The gravel is neat.
There's a sheen in the grooves of
The sloped, curving roof.
Visiting, I feel clean, like
A newly printed bank note.

四

The other side of
The beauty, health and comfort:
My bowels pinned with dread.
My shit feels worse, looks worse, smells
Worse than back home in England.

五

Toriniku sees
The pack of Wakaba we
Bought on the table
Where we're eating gyôza, and
Remarks, "*Metcha shibui!*"

六

So much unfolds in
Silence. The silence that first
Disappoints, unfolds
Into something greater than
Expected. Kawai's house.

7th November

—

Outside the bathroom
Window, collecting car fumes,
Something like hedge, or
Something like tree, is not, yet
Is Japan's blade-like tension.

=

I step from the mouth
Of an alley and there, like
A city-crunching
Godzilla, wooden, unreal,
A five-storey pagoda.

≡

The stone steps—shallow,
Shelving—of Yasaka Shrine,
Though worn by many
Feet, are clean, like the glaze of
Pottery, indented, smooth.

8th November

—

From the next room, I
Hear the squeal of a zip on
A travelling case.
Outside, the many-layered
Sound of rain. Farewell, Kyôto.

=

Dusk is brief here. At
5 p.m., the cold glitter
Of passing streets from
The window of a bus. Warm
Resignation of darkness.

9th November

—

Because I feel I'm
Changing—that's why I want to
Live longer. If I
Died now, people would know me
For who I no longer am.

=

Into the raining
Night on the express. Alleys
Gape, signs lit up with
The same old invitations
To stop. Travel—sweet as death.

≡

Like the charming clouds
That everyone knows, folds of
Discarded clothing
Recur in Japanese art;
Kafû dwells on them in prose.

四

So, while Bee-chan sleeps,
With the dull, autumn light of
Noon on hydrangea
And tatami, I think of
Those discarded clothes, and write.

五

A reservation
At the Shimizuya Inn.
The landlord shows us,
At the desk, the wi-fi code,
And Bee-chan takes a photo.

10th November

一

The straight, rising road
To Zenkôji. On both sides,
Wooden lanterns, red
Leaves. We share the umbrella
From Ôsaka, mid-journey.

二

A pine with mossy
Roots in the tiny courtyard
Garden. Breakfast in
Yukata, then back to bed:
To our room in Nagano.

三

The repose of a
Mid-sized town. We do little,
Gladly. The journey
Layers here; music whose theme
Repeats, varies, develops.

四

Always some people
Declare: if it's real, it's free;
A temple entrance
Fee proves it's fake. But actors,
Persisting, become sincere.

五

Taking a photo
Of a row of stone lanterns,
I don't mind, these days,
The sign for the toilets. But,
I take another without.

六

A satchel-red train.
We get off at Obusé.
A white-gloved guard stands
At the door. A whistle blows—
This air, soft as the water.

七

An illustration
Shows the Snow Monkey Express
Stops here. Autumn-patched
Mountains, the view's terminus.
We cross the tracks to exit.

八

Hokusai drew all things
From the soap opera of
Merchants to cosmic
Waterfalls. The lightness is
The depth: portrait, landscape, space.

九

Kurita Bookshop.
The tinny doors rattle in
Their grooves. But it's here,
Not the big place, that stocks the
Book I want: *Ukigumo*.

11th November

—

Our Morishigé
Lodgings depressed you. The name:
'Overgrown forest'.
The furnishings are old and
Funky. Your funk here was blue.

二

Hokusai, near the end,
Did nothing but paint. His home
Filled with packaging
From takeaways. What kind of
Takeaways? Broiled eel, perhaps.

三

Sendai seen from the
Shinkansen platform: the same
Metal plating as
Anywhere in Japan—a
Blind pulled down on history.

12th November

—

A sentimental
Song piped from somewhere on a
Drizzly street corner.
A period-drama theme,
It means: life's a little stream.

二

The *Manyôshû* notes
Explain: back then, names were thought
To have their own souls.
At Poppo-no-Ashiyu,
Bathing my feet, I agree.

三

The corridor in
Our lodgings forms a zig-zag
Like a boardwalk. At
One corner, a space heater,
A microwave, some lumber.

13th November

—

The gift-wrapping seems
To make up for everything.
Like an end-credits
Scene, a train crossing a gorge.
Inside, Naruko mushrooms.

=

Entsûin. In haste
I leave the lit-up autumn
Viewing and wait for
The train inside the station
Building, less cold than outside.

≡

On the third floor, a
Cosy, grungy café. A
Little rocking horse
Under the piano. I
Bet it's never been ridden.

14th November

—

I expect: steep streets
Overlooking a Hokusai
Sea, dark kawara
Roofs, a stern, feudal pathos.
I get: bad jazz and omelette.

二

The taxi ride through
Tochigi to Nasu Zoo
Was like a drive through
Devon, but the undergrowth
Was emptiness and bamboo.

三

The lemurs made one
Wide ball of hugs; you couldn't
Count them. Outside, an
Enclosure contained dogs for
Stroking—now please wash your hands.

四

The Kamakura
Daibutsu is one case where
Sheer size seems sublime.
The umbrellas of tourists
Cluster round like lotus leaves.

五

At Rokujizô
Bus stop, two young ladies in
Kimono, two shades
Of pink, alight, and put up
Two umbrellas. Pink again.

六

Seidensticker says
Kafû's lovers are always
Dry and rustling, but
He neglects to mention that
They're shibui and funky.

七

In Kamakura,
We listen to Kodagain's
'Kamakura' while
Walking in the rain, like a
Karaoke video.

15th November

一

Just arrived. Smoking
On the verandah of our
Sendai lodgings with
A rock-garden view of coiled
Parts of disembowelled buildings.

二

Six-twenty something
At Kuki Station. Less than
Thirty minutes till
Our connection. Phone ahead,
Buy mints, rush to the platform.

16th November

一

Ôta-shi at night.
Walking back home, at a bend
In the road, bats from
Ujigami Shrine. Believe
And you make a shrine for bats.

25

二

Feathery bamboo,
Then mountains shawled with russet,
Grey, beige, yellow, rust.
Autumn dyes dried deep and fine.
Slopes tufted with susuki.

三

Illumination.
"Flower fantasy." Light shows
Here are like the cakes:
White-flour nothings, barely
Food, with rococo toppings.

17th November

一

For instance, the sun
Like peeling gold leaf on the
River just before
Iwajuku—too many
Moments like this to write down.

二

The world after cars:
That moonlight glint on the stream
Beneath the concrete
Bridge we passed in poignant ease,
Now we must walk by slowly.

三

The boy kicked his heels,
Capered, on the train. Questioned
By his mother, he
Protested, "I was doing
An *omoshiroi* dance."

四

"The house keys!" she said.
The driver she'd ordered made
A stoic U-turn,
Reporting to H.Q. by
Radio: "U-turn. U-turn."

五

A mountain temple.
Dusk. Talk of local things. The
Barrier we saw
Was not to protect us from
Landslides, but from wild boar.

六

Unfortunately,
The Café de Paris was
Closing in thirty
Minutes. I left. Then came back.
"Tomorrow?" I asked. "We're closed."

七

The colours begin
To run with alcohol. As
Time passes so you
Begin to doubt free will; you
Float in warm resignation.

八

A tall building seen
From a taller. One lighted
Cell with curtains drawn.
A thin crack remains, fingers
Visible at a keyboard.

九

Haze obliterates
The outlines of the building
So what remains are
Lights like lines of type, credits
Floating on unscrolling night.

18th November

一

Poetry's a thing
Of such high definition
You can keep zooming
In, endlessly. This is how
We slow time. Forget drama.

二

As forecast, rain. We
Pick up the key Justin left
And get in the flat.
I smoke on the balcony.
Umbrellas pass Lawson's glow.

三

Tôkyô revs without
Pause. Vast agitation that
Becomes harmony
On which see-through umbrellas
Float like spindly jellyfish.

19ᵗʰ November

—

James's flat reminds
Me of exchange-student days:
Space-capsule genkan,
Snacks and drinks, a vast screen, and
Nationhood amputated.

二

Post-karaoke,
Sleeping late, daylight on stained
Bedding. Under a
Hello Kitty bed-sheet, like
A mouse in sawdust—J-bon.

三

Kabuki-chô, at
Café de Bore, I waited
For you. The 'cake set'
Was expensive. You came and
When we left it poured and poured.

29

20th November

一

Going for a piss,
I leave the booth, and pass the
Numbered doors. Music
Muted now. Off-key singing
Like sleep-talk from separate worlds.

二

They play 'Auld Lang Syne'
To close the museum. We
Linger. When we leave,
My umbrella is the last,
Left locked in the tiered rack.

三

On the Zushi train,
Just past Yokohama, we
Come to a place where
Buildings limpet on crooked
Slopes shaggy with weeds and trees.

四

Ten thousand worlds pray
For peace. Fulfilment of this
Wish looks easy to
The Great Buddha of Hasé.
Fear makes future; peace is now.

21st November

—

Strange, long-snouted fish
Hang from the ceiling of the
Izakaya. Seas
Near exhausted, weirder and
Weirder fish are harvested.

二

An izakaya
In Shimo-Kitazawa,
The bill of fare on
Separate wooden tablets tiles
The wall, cleanly unvarnished.

三

Like the gluey taste
Of the saké my father
Brought back from Japan,
The flight-pack slippers he gave
Me were imbued with glamour.

22nd November

—

Fine weather for our
Departure. Early morning
Tôkyô, like a drive
Through an architect's model.
Fire escapes—fish bones picked clean.

23rd November

—

Smell is memory's
Forgotten sense. We stopped at
A rattling roadside
Shop and paraffin made the
Space heater a time machine.

=

In both Naruko
And Kusatsu, wind wafted
Sulphur, we ate bad
Soba, and paraffin brought
Back the heart of my Japan.

24th November

—

Now the trip is done,
I grow sad with the joy of
The moments that are
Gone. Fondly, I hear you say,
"These pickles are a nightmare."

25th November

—

The farthest north we
Went: Naruko. We climbed steep
Shrine steps, stars fresh as
Spray above the steam. The shrine
Was dark. We turned back and kissed.

二

In our small room in
Kamakura, I massaged
You in the blueish
T.V. glow. A samisen
Played notes of swift, silent snow.

三

At the shrine halfway
Through our hike, the ema were
Shaped like hearts, and I
Thought of Swizzels Love Hearts and
Believed in childish wishes.

Zuihitsu
随筆

A Sense of Unhome

For many years I have wanted to write about Japan, but despite the considerable investment I have made in Japan-related study and in locating periods of my life in the country, I have been unable to. I noticed, from the nineties, if not before, a rash of books selling — it appeared — reasonably well, whose authors were simply westerners who had lived in Japan and wanted to talk about the experience. For me there was a frustration, perhaps more like anguish, in contemplating this phenomenon, since what I had to talk about, if I spoke about Japan, was a kind of vacuum. It wasn't an experience — it was a non-experience, or even an anti-experience. At best, when there were positive experiences, in both senses of the word, they seemed either so slight or so ineffable as to resist expression in writing, though to me, paradoxically, they were rich and nuanced, possessing a consistent texture and significance. Such experiences would include watching steam rise from green tea or seeing sun stream through the ears of the susuki in autumn. It is significant that in the first example, the setting does not ultimately matter. The Japan I was expecting to find—the natural and historical Japan—before I came, has been so much obliterated under ugly modern urbanisation, that the ability to focus on the faintest manifestations of beauty—like the enfeebled but ever-returning ghosts of animistic deities—is necessarily cultivated in anyone who sincerely loves Japanese culture. The cup of green tea in question might simply be placed on the greasy floor of a garage where a car is being repaired, but, to the right eyes, that steam will transform the surroundings into a mystical brocade manifesting the true Japanese spirit.

There is a kind of essentialist faith in this, which some might find absurd. Fundamentally, it means that, although the spirit of Japan might be successfully evoked anywhere, all else being equal, a cup of sencha in Japan is always a more authentic conduit of the Japanese spirit than a cup of sencha anywhere else. Or, to put it another way—and perhaps I shall convert this into a tanka—the difference between a *Tonari no Totoro* fabric cover for a toilet-roll holder in Japan and the same fabric cover for a toilet-roll holder anywhere else in the world is that if you have seen the former, you have been given the chance to experience for yourself the spirit of Japan, in such a direct manner that you might legitimately claim 'culture shock' as a result, whereas, if you have seen the latter, you have merely had the chance to allow the spirit of Japan to be evoked for you in such a way that you might wish to travel there yourself for access to the direct experience. But is this some-would-say-absurd idea true? I will be unequivocal: yes, it is. This leap of faith is a core premise of this current book. Taking it, you will find many subtleties of human existence becoming available to you. That is, you are liberated by a Parmenidean revelation that everything, simply, *is*. I already know the objection to this assertion. If everything is, then why are some things more Japanese than others? But I didn't say everything *is Japanese*. We grant there is an essence of Japan. Without distinctions, we can't grant such essences. Besides, I'm not so much making an argument for a theory as a practice, and for what that practice makes possible. To be able to accept that there is an essence to Japanese culture means being able to treat the ineffable as objective reality. Without this method of levelling all reality so that one can open it up as one pleases like a sectioned paintbox, one is always deferring to confusion and will remain at the bottom of a top-down universe. But I am afraid that I am becoming too continental in tone. I will illustrate my meaning and hope that what is obscure will become clear.

I am fascinated when ineffable experiences recur, as this suggests to me that, although they might have no name, they have an objective existence—as colours do—and can therefore be studied. Poetry explores precisely this territory. A formulation of words from one mind seems sometimes able to create the same experience again and again in other minds.

I will give some biographical information now— that is, recount some memories—to provide a foil of understanding against which such experiences can occur for and be recognised by the reader. The memories in question belong to the period of eighteen months, from October, 2001, to March, 2003, during which I lived in Kyôto and studied at the Faculty of Letters in Kyôto University.

This was a very lonely period of my life, the period at which, I believe, I became fully cognisant of the fact that loneliness can reach such a pitch that it is indistinguishable from fear. I had experienced this before, certainly—an *uncanny* loneliness—but this very simple truth, that fear and loneliness can be the same thing, had somehow never crystallised for me until then. I believe this loneliness was also instrumental in shaping my aesthetic sensibilities, in relation to Japan and to the world in general. The reader might wonder why I was so lonely. I am not sure there is a simple answer. I noticed, however, the feelings that would suddenly awaken in me at the chance hearing of an English accent on a train. Cultural background makes more difference, I realised, than I had been led to believe. There were so many things that I would not have to explain to a compatriot. Besides, I was a transient here. Why should anyone care about me? I am very much predisposed to loneliness, anyway, and Japan, to me, seemed to impose an icy, airless suffocation of the spirit. I might have been in space, deprived of all those small but meaningful moments of human contact that occur even on an unremarkable day when one is in a familiar environment. Sure enough, I spoke to people, but I got little sense that I was treated as human in such interactions.

It was in precisely this vacuum that, to give an example, I became very interested in Japanese ceramics. With a kind of wrench of perversity and beauty, I found the feelings that normally would be channelled into human interaction instead focused on the chill delicacy of a teacup, the curve of its bowl cut perfectly at the rim of its mouth, its smooth, glazed sides decorated with pale blue flowers. I am describing one of my favourite pieces—a very cheap piece, in fact. There were many others, however, either that I bought, or that I felt my heart break over because I knew there must be a limit to my buying, and because I knew, as I might know of someone I loved, that however I stared and caressed, I could not finally possess them because I could not become them.

I rode up and down the thoroughfares of Kyôto searching out the many shops selling ceramics. They were the object of a kind of emergency to me. They were a life-line preventing me from suffocating entirely through lack of meaning. And so the reader, I believe, may easily discern how this became a training in aesthetic sensitivity. I was thrown in at the deep end of panicky loneliness, and aesthetic appreciation of delicate details and atmospheres—to which, I think, I already had some inclination—became my only means of swimming.

I remember the curious shock with which, some years before, I had first read Fujiwara no Okikaze's tanka in the poetry collection the *Ogura Hyakunin Isshu*. The poem runs:

> *Tare wo ka mo*
> *Shiru hito ni semu*
> *Takasago no*
> *Matsu mo mukashi no*
> *Tomo naranaku ni.*

> Who is there left
> Who knows me from those long gone
> Days? The pines at
> Takasago beach still stand,
> But they are not my friends.

I saw in my mind the pine—symbol of long life—at which the poet gazed. I felt his loneliness before this magnificence. What was it to him? Why did the splendid pines still stand and what could they mean when he, outliving his friends, had lived too long? And yet I sensed, beneath the loneliness, a strange vibrancy, perhaps that thing that has been called 'mono no awaré', because, even in the cold strangeness of this world without friends, the pine, speechless, dumbfounding, is, after all, alive, and—speechless, dumbfounding, alive—is a kind of mirror to the poet himself. He, like the pines, still stands. He, like the pines in that, surely has a silent splendour.

In other words, the poem was both shock and consolation.

So it was for me, in Kyôto, with my obsession, in my loneliness, for ceramics. What could they mean to me? And yet, they told me there was a world still, and that my heart and these ceramics were part of it. If I were to die, the next day the sun would rise upon that world. There was comfort in this. I would pass though the world did not, yet my passing heart was attuned to pieces of fragile beauty in that world.

I can tell more about the loneliness I felt in Kyôto—a great deal more. I will tell some; perhaps too much.

After staying with a Japanese family for a while in Yamashina, a southeastern suburb of Kyôto, I spent a number of months in a newly built dormitory in Ôbaku, somewhat farther out, though still part of Kyôto Prefecture. Though a completed building, the dormitory barely escaped the feeling of being a volume of concrete, planking and other cheap materials

42

slapped together according to a template of the greatest convenience for the builders and intended to do nothing more than store a number of living spaces on top of each other. My room was tiny, but at least it had an en-suite bathroom—a windowless, plastic space capsule of the kind familiar to residents of Japan. It had a bed, a sink, a single electric plate for cooking, and a small balcony. It was on this balcony that I spent much of my time—brooding, I would say, except that, to me, the word has a settled sound, and I was very unsettled. I had nowhere to go, no one to meet, I was thousands of miles from home and my life was leaking away in vain like water from a punctured bag. When the loneliness got too much for me—a confining cage in which I struggled—I would go out on to the balcony and smoke a cigarette or two. I consoled myself by choosing to smoke Wakaba—the name means 'young leaves'—which to me looked like the kind of cigarette old Japanese geezers might have smoked in some unidentifiable period of the past, new enough to be captured on film, but old enough for people to have lived primarily with people, so that the world was composed of first-person experience, conversation and rumour.

Ôbaku is next to—perhaps one could say 'part of'—Uji. There is an Ôbaku school of Zen and Uji is a name notable in Japanese literature. In the *Ogura Hyakunin Isshu*, another poet, Kisen Hôshi, tells of his retreat to a hut in Ujiyama (Uji Mountain), far from the capital. Instead of people, he has deer for company. The Ôbaku dormitory was built on a hill, but if this was 'Ujiyama' it no longer offered the benefits of wilderness, only the loneliness and the fear that come with backwater

43

obscurity. The view had little to recommend it, but at least I had physical elevation here and something of that sense of detached panorama that the word 'view' suggests and the act of viewing can bring. Smoking, looking out over the landscape so poignantly ruined by the roads and supermarkets, the economically determined rubbish of modernisation, I believe I was trying to ferment the content of my inner experience to the kind of resolution that the artist requires for creativity and that humans, generally, require in order to feel that they have lived. But I smoked, I gazed and I paced and this resolution, this sense of adding up to something, eluded me. I was isolated in an absence, a lack, a sense of unhome, that has come to characterise much of my experience of Japan.

Student life in England had been very much a communal matter, though there had been plenty of nights of jagged loneliness for me even then. The lack of community I experienced in student life in Japan was eerie—ghostly, even. Naturally, I tried to assuage my loneliness by socialising with the other students in the dormitory, most of whom, like me, were foreign to Japan and who therefore might have been expected to be inclined to foster camaraderie. But for some reason, my attempts failed absolutely. There was a common room, with a television, on the ground floor of the dormitory. On a number of occasions I came down to this space when sounds indicated the presence of others, in the hope, first of all, that I might pass some minutes less painfully than usual, and secondly, that I might even make friends. Although I did manage to speak to one or two of the other students, it was quite as if I spoke to no one. I am not even sure how to describe the sensation. An old Japanese saying has it that, "Two sleeves brushing is karma from another life." In other words, even when you pass someone in the street, this is a sign your lives are cosmically linked. I felt, however, that there had never been and never would be a life in which I was linked with these people. It was not even antipathy. For that matter, I only felt good will, tepid though it was, towards them. It was as though I was talking to the television. The students seemed to me as inaccessible and two-dimensional as figures on a T.V. screen. The television, perhaps, was haunting the common room, and that was all. Or perhaps—I inevitably began to feel—it was I who was the ghost.

As pain makes it hard to keep still, so did my loneliness. I tried many things, hopelessly, one after the other, to soothe and distract myself. Often, I would go for walks. I am afraid these were mostly mechanical, as if I were simply pacing up and down, but doing it outdoors, in wide circuits, instead of in my room.

However, something was to happen to me during these circuits of Ôbaku that was quite to move me, and which I am sure I shall never forget. It was usually as I was walking along the pavement, where weeds curled in the mesh of a wire fence, near the dormitory itself. Coming from the opposite direction I would see a shambling, unwashed figure—a man perhaps in his fifties, who appeared to be a habitual drinker and might also have been homeless. I am afraid I never learnt who he was. He would stop when he became aware of me. As he tended to look at the ground as he shuffled along, he would not be far distant, but perhaps forty paces or so away, or nearer. He would stop, and look up at me with an expression that I struggle

45

to articulate, of mixed surprise and recognition. But most of all, there was a clear impact of my presence—there was no doubt that at last I had been seen. He would raise his hand and hail me, and I would return the greeting. Then we would continue, each on his own way. Another human being had seen me, had recognised me, and so, I felt, I must be human, too, and the blood became warmer in my veins, and I was saved from fading entirely into the empty chill of ghosthood.

Mostly, though, it is precisely that chill I remember. I felt as if the same chill of spirit had occupied the country for thousands of years, that the terrible, bleak fatalism of Japanese literature and art through history spoke always of the essential loneliness of a watchman, awake through an icy night, with no hope of human warmth, only haunted by resentful ghosts, but afraid to ignore the demands of duty and abandon his post, speechless, terrified, anguished, as a tendril of mist crept across the ground towards him, hissing with all the concentrated inhumanity of the headless world of self-sacrifice into which he was born.

I, myself, visualised that ancient tendril of mist, I heard it hiss, felt the iciness of its approach, when I walked around Ôbaku at night, knowing there was no one to whom I could disclose the thoughts and feelings in my heart.

On one such night, I saw something that amazed me. The dormitory was near to the temple, Manpukuji, which I believe is the historical seat of the Ôbaku school of Zen, and what I saw must have been a part of the temple. A turret or upper room was lit, and stood out in the night as if it were a scene on the theatre stage.

The shutters of the room were wide open and there was no glass to divide the interior from the outside. The whole night seemed to share in the intimacy of that chamber — an intimacy, it seemed, in which the sound of a pen dropping on the matted floor could have been heard. In that room was a shaven-headed priest wearing ceremonial robes. He knelt before a great drum, the skin of which was presented vertically, so that it resembled a gong. The priest beat upon this drum slowly, at first, but powerfully, with a naturalness that was also a kind of perfection. Never did a stroke sound mistimed, never too weak or too strong, though the strokes speeded up and gathered strength. The turret was surrounded, outside, by darkness, but the drum glowed with the yellow of the interior light, so that it was as if the priest was beating the moon with his stick, and the moon's solemn thunder was speaking through the dark.

I stood and watched — stood as if there were nothing left of me but watching and listening. The beating of the drum seemed to go on for a long time, but in a rare defeat of time, there was no exhaustion, in the sight, the sound, or in me. This was not the polyphony of church bells, just one man, one stick, one drum, and yet I was captivated by that irregular beating, cresting and lulling like waves, as I have never been by the melodious art of the bell-ringers.

Eventually, the beating thundered to a climax of a kind often attempted in various forms of music, but seldom achieved. It was done. The priest, with an abrupt rattle and snap, closed the shutters that hid the room from view, as if thereby ending a ceremony.

I realised then that I had seen something, heard

something, experienced something. There had been no words and I would not have known at the time how to explain and value it in words. In Japan's icy darkness, down history, there had been moments like this—inexplicable, beautiful moments. I understood something then of Japanese art, Japanese spirituality. The enchantment of everyday objects. The eerie beauty and brevity of the tanka. That light in the darkness, that drum, that wordlessness, that snapping of shutters—from this I had gained, though I did not at first realise it, precisely that sense of resolution I had needed.

That was not the last time I stood in the Ôbaku night, watching and listening to the drumming of the priest in the turret room. Always alone in that room, always open to the night, in that strange mix of distance and intimacy, always in harmony with the tension of the drum, he would bring the beating to a thunderous climax and swiftly bring the shutters closed with a final rattle and snap.

Such occasions were a great consolation to me. The austerity of the scene was a kindness imparting to me strange wealth and luxury.

By such means I was ushered into the secret inner sanctum of my own relationship with Japan. It is from that inner sanctum that I am now attempting to bring tidings and souvenirs.

I will unwrap the delicate paper packaging and offer you—moments. That is what I have learnt and brought back from Japan. There are many things you can do with such moments, but let me tell you about a game you can play with them, just in case you need a suggestion.

I did have friends in Kyôto, in fact. One thing I have learnt in life is that such things as loneliness cannot be mathematically calculated. My feelings have puzzled me because I so seldom find anything like them represented in the world. Yet here I am, the centre of the world, as far as I am concerned, and as obscure to the world whose centre I constitute as if I had been born invisible.

Anyway, this is not the place for that old lament. I did have friends. I shall talk about one of them here, and I shall give him the false name Boris Jeffries. Boris was an unusual person, quite playful in conversation, with a distinct, almost cruel streak of snobbishness the like of which I had not encountered before; he was good company when he chose to be, but for at least part of our time in Kyôto he chose not to keep company with me. He told me himself that he had been deliberately ignoring me. I was, after this brief spell in Coventry, reinstated, a little uneasily, as . . . perhaps, after all, he did not think of me as a friend, but he deigned to spend time with me and be agreeable again until we returned to Britain, and for a little while after that. We are no longer in touch, though he is certainly a memorable figure for me when I look back over the years that have passed.

Boris, like me, was English, and, like me, was studying Japanese literature on a postgraduate scholarship at Kyôto University. We flew over on the same plane, meeting for the first time in the airport lounge where we waited for our flight. We struck up a friendship immediately, almost as if we were friends already. I remember that, at that very first meeting, he looked out of the lounge windows at an aeroplane coming in to land and said, "Amazing, isn't it? I don't understand people who stop finding these things amazing." And so I was impressed at the beginning with the sense that here was someone with a living heart, capable of wonder, than which, I think, there might be no greater qualification for friendship.

Boris was restless, lively and enterprising, and always full of well-researched suggestions for outings, activities and so on. He would find me in the campus canteen, or phone me up, and say, "Come on, let's go on a hike to Kurama," or, "I've discovered a great little place to eat on Pontochô; let's go there." On one such occasion, it was a shop specialising in incense that he had discovered. He enquired whether I was interested in incense and, finding I was, suggested an expedition (the shop was in a strange part of town, to the north and quite removed from the commercial centre).

I remember the shop as occupying the first floor of a building containing other commercial premises, and having a fashionable, converted-warehouse feel to it. I also remember it being a relatively large space, at least considering the small scale of the goods being sold. Yet, in my memory, most of that large space is a blank. There might have been shelves upon shelves of more or less traditional incense lining the walls, but the image that remains with me is this: by or on the counter there was a Perspex display case in the form of a grid of cubes, with each cube containing a tiny stick of incense and, on a piece of paper stuck to the back of the cube, a number accompanied by a description or designation. The varieties of incense here did not have names—they had numbers. Or rather, their names were like the names of some cocktails, and numbers were therefore necessary for convenience or, perhaps, to spare the more diffident customers embarrassment. If I try to recall, now, specific number-and-name combinations, what comes to mind are things like: #27, weekly piano lesson, or #89, meeting a friend at the aquarium.

We bought incense together here only once or twice, but it was this shop that formed the basis of one of our conversational games. Looking back, I am struck by the childlike playfulness in which we spontaneously cooperated even in the midst of despondency. I miss such idleness.

It was a simple matter. Whenever we were inspired to do so—and preferably in the middle of a conversation to which the inspiration bore no relation—we were to intone, declaim, or otherwise interject, "Number forty-three, last week's password", or "Number seventeen, badly grazed knee", or, "Number one hundred and two, a comparison of hats", or "Number ninety-four, explaining to your neighbour that you lost the bicycle pump he lent you three weeks ago", or whatever other self-contained image, concept or scenario came to mind. There were even rules, though they were not fixed. I don't remember all of them, only that the name of the scent must not be too dramatic and, as Boris insisted, it should in no way suggest any actual scent or provide a clue by which one could even imagine a scent. I confess I found this last rule a little hard. I always wanted a teasing possibility of scent there. I wanted to think to myself, now what would *that* smell like? Boris, I think, revelled in the absurdity of sheer olfactory impasse. But perhaps it was a similar position. What is the sound of one hand clapping? What is the smell of leaving your umbrella on the Snow Monkey Express?

And so, although the game I played with Boris was the epitome of uselessness, was irrelevance *par excellence*, was, to employ a phrase that might only be understood by a handful of British readers, entirely hatstand, and although I did not realise it at the time, it provided me with another tool for processing experience, complementary to the tool that had been passed on to me by the drumming priest.

Number forty-four, a priest beats a single, moon-bright drum alone in the Ôbaku night.

On the 1st of November, 2015, Bee-chan and I arrived at Kansai Airport, Japan, after a two-leg flight via Istanbul, taking, altogether, somewhere in the region of thirteen hours. It was evening when we arrived, though for us it was something like the morning after a sleepless night.

Airports are strange, in-between zones. You might say, for instance: "I've never been to Hong Kong. Well, I didn't set foot outside the airport." It is as if, in airports, all countries are nullified. I have often been troubled, at airports, by the question of how far this nullification is a fact and how far merely a prejudice or illusion. In any case, it often seems a shame that arrival in a country must start with something as drab and neutral as an airport. At least the various gates manage to give something of the theatre of entrance and exit. But when does the entrance really begin?

It was, I believe, my sixth time in Japan, Bee-chan's third. For me, there was a mixed sense of anticipating discovery and anticipating deepening familiarity, or more blankly, simple reacquaintance. To put it another way, I wondered to myself, how will Japan be this time?

It was a relief to be at the airport, but there my sense of having returned to Japan was minimal. From the airport, we needed to take a train to Ôsaka, where we had a room booked for the night at the Swiss Hotel. The pleasures of familiarity began for me with the purchase of train tickets. I did not have my bearings immediately, but I was not lost or bewildered. I felt myself adjusting to Japanese local information again quickly.

We boarded a train. Here, exhaustion, relief and flat familiarity began to stew together in a strange recipe of tepid emotion. Again the question came: How will Japan be this time?

I began to be aware of that indefinable impression of absence that Japan had so often given me before. I will make some attempt to describe it. Things surely cannot be more or less than they are. We look around, and reality is precisely the fullness of itself, self-measuring, like a cup so full it cannot be moved without spillage, but exactly and only full and not in any sense overflowing. This is how a house is precisely a house, filling its designated space and leaving no vacuum, and a person is precisely a person and so on. And yet, in Japan, I have often felt an actual absence, a concavity, a deficit, as if reality itself has been eaten away by termites and therefore doesn't fill the exact outline it should.

One can entertain and discard all sorts of theories as to the causes of this impression, but for me, whatever the cause, the impression itself recurs. As I became accustomed, on that train, to my deep fatigue, as if my eyes were adjusting to darkness, my mind brought into focus, quite distinctly, in my surroundings, the abovementioned absence, familiar from past experience. Again, the question: What is it, exactly? I don't know for sure, but it is something like a terrible sense of unhome, as if humanity has lost the keys to its own house and can't get back in; as if social repression has restrained reality itself so powerfully as to deform it, with the rationalisation always and ever that this shrunken, tortured thing, like a bonsai, is a sophisticated culture.

Well, often enough, the rationalisation persuades me. (How else could I bear to be English?)

I must have said something to Bee-chan about my impressions, but I do not remember what. She asked if I was tired of coming to Japan, if I would have preferred to go somewhere else. No, not at all, I reassured her. Between myself and Japan there was 'en'—karmic connection.

Because I have a habit of constant analysis of impressions, I think I can sometimes make observations that are meant to express a point of interest but which are received by the listener as barbs. In fact, I was slowly bringing into full operation those sensibilities I had developed in order to appreciate Japan. Foreigners who have never visited Japan have quite a limited set of images by which to conjure the country to themselves. I hardly dare list the clichés, though in the right context they can be pleasing. Zen merges

54

with electronics by way of geisha. Such images are a gift for those who work in advertising. However, what they obscure is the extent to which Japan has historically been a country of farmers (who were traditionally of higher status than artisans and traders), and the extent to which Japan is, even now, rural in many of its mannerisms, social relations and in much of its residual atmosphere. It is a country of slightly dodgy but kindly old geezers and of aggressively polite aunties in aprons.

The train in which we travelled could have been one of those in which I rode the first time I came to Japan, back in the nineteen nineties. It was quite the same feeling as if I were visiting a school I used to attend and was recognised by the caretaker, who proceeded to take me into some little shed that he occupied — and which I also remembered — to offer me a cup of badly brewed tea and some stale biscuits. He would be wearing the same, familiar overalls as always and would look no older than he ever had, because he had ever been rickety, sunken-cheeked and grizzled. And once we were both sitting, he would make oddly uncomfortable attempts at conversation, and together we would not be able to do much to break the back of the silence, and yet I would not want to leave, but would feel, in my heart, some obscure gladness as if something wonderful had happened, though, there being no explanation for it, the feeling would fade like a dream.

The hotel was immediately above the train station. It took a while to pay for our room, for technical reasons to do with the deposit, but eventually we were escorted in the lift to our room on the top floor. We looked out of the window at the nighted city. Steel, glass and concrete stretched to the horizon, with not a hint of anything organic except the human inhabitants and with no sense that anything visible here was older than those inhabitants. There seemed no history except for that of those still living; no memory except living memory. Electric lights made the city look like one vast, motionless pinball game. The buildings had the chrome look of cars—polished, new—almost plastic in their lack of character. The night air, where the darkness was dissolved a little by the radiance, had a sheen of purple to it, as if the atmosphere itself were alienated from the natural world.

This, after all, was something like the Japan known to foreigners—the sleek modernity—even if it did not have quite the aesthetic qualifications for an advertising poster.

The room was deluxe in an anonymous way. We wondered whether simply to go to bed, or whether to go out first for an evening meal. We decided on a nap, then a meal. Dead dark. Dead weight of blankets. Dead sleep of dead exhaustion. Then the alarm. If anything, I felt dizzier, stranger, not refreshed. Nonetheless, I was somehow ready and eager to set out in search of somewhere to eat.

Bee-chan didn't want to go too far from our hotel, though now we were out on the street I quite wanted to stretch my legs and explore a little. On the other hand, she was right: it would be good to eat soon, and have a little drink and relax. But we remained indecisive about where. For some reason, despite hunger and tiredness, we were both feeling a little bit choosy. It was one of those periods of dissatisfaction that seem to occur for no very good reason intermittently when one is on holiday. We went down one street, up another and then back the way we had come. We said, "If we don't find a better place on the next street, we'll come back to this place," and then we came back and almost went in but decided, after all, to look just a little longer. Noodles would be fine, but then again, I'd rather have something else. We passed and considered tiny, narrow izakayas that were too cramped but, on the other hand, looked authentic. There were brash lights as of amusement arcades, vermilion paper lanterns and shop signs, massage parlours with signs outside on the pavement, the general bric-a-brac of Japanese nightlife.

In the end, we did not enter any of the places we said we would come back to. As often happens in these situations, we saw somewhere new just as we were tiring beyond tolerance of our search. It was not the most promising place we had seen, perhaps, but it would do. Glass frontage showed a more spacious interior than some of the places we had seen, and it also seemed, for that reason, perhaps a touch less traditional and a touch more bland. I was not sure of the menu, either, but with our decision made, I experienced the satisfaction of sliding into an effortless resignation.

We entered and sat at the counter. For some reason, as we did so, a strange, almost mystical confidence began to glow within me. I looked at the menu and asked if Bee-chan trusted me to order. She said she did.

Muscles disused for some time had, nonetheless, not atrophied. I tested them, and they responded.

I ordered beer and edamame. Casting my eye over the menu, I saw exactly the fish I was looking for—buri (Japanese amberjack). I also ordered aji shioyaki (salted horse makerel) and shishamo (willow-leaf fish). I was in Japan again, and nothing now would prevent me from ordering all manner of fish. I believe I ordered other dishes, too, but I cannot now recall what they were.

The counter staff cooked and served our food as we watched, and asked us in a polite but quietly genial way where we were from, what we were doing here, all the usual questions. They are entirely predictable questions, of course, but on this occasion they felt as pleasant as a moderately firm massage.

The aji shioyaki was placed on the counter for us—whole from head to tail, on a rectangular ceramic dish (perhaps in the bizen-yaki style), a small pyramid of finely grated white radish on its silvery, salted skin, and a slice of lemon at its side. Such moments, though we seldom express them, are satisfying beyond compare.

The alcohol was beginning to circulate in my bloodstream and Bee-chan, it seemed, was enjoying the meal. There was a moment when, with gladness, I knew that the feeling of absence was gone. Japan also has these moments of richness—luxurious and sub-tle. I am tempted to say that I am better able to enjoy them now because I have learnt a little what I secretly suspect many Japanese have long since mastered—the trick of how to make one's home in the unhome.

I felt no unease about the first chunk taken from my holiday budget by this meal.

We did not hurry, but did not linger. When we paid the bill and left, we stepped out into the evening air as if into our own mellowness and found that a few gentle spots of rain were falling through the warm atmosphere. We must have stopped and looked up. The young man who had been serving us hurried out with an umbrella and opened it for us—it was large enough for two, with a tartan pattern. I made to refuse it, but he insisted, and so, gratefully, I accepted, and we walked away beneath it together, back to our hotel.

In the morning, when it was light, we looked out at the cityscape from our top-floor room once more. Now we could see what had been invisible in the darkness—trees lining some of the grey avenues, looking, from this distance, like the green, plastic boscage around the edges of a train set.

Tourism

At Kawai Kanjirô's house I noticed an objective stillness—that is, a stillness, I believe, consistently noticed
by others, too. Appropriately, it was a stillness apparent in the form of objects—the old furnishings, the
ceramic pieces, wooden carvings and so on. I flipped
open a book early on, apparently of Kanjirô's writings.
My eye rested on a line to the effect that people now are
not accustomed to turning themselves into "mono"—
things—and that thought remains ineffectual until
they do. Kanjirô wrote epigrams in calligraphy. 手考
足思. "Hands ponder. Feet think." Or perhaps it is an
exhortation.

I began to feel kinship with Kanjirô. The silence he
had bequeathed the world somehow contained within
it that experience that belongs to no religion, though
all claim it as their own and none would exist without
it, of an intuited benevolence intrinsic to existence.
The experience for me is occasional. No—it's impos-
sible to measure frequency. It seems sometimes near
and sometimes far. At the times when it is near it has
about it the sense of a promise, that the benevolence

will unfold in my own life. I am never sure whether to take this literally. "The butterfly takes wing; the leaves take wing." Another of Kanjirô's epigrams. In other words, the leaves are devastated by caterpillars, but in being thus devastated, the leaves themselves become butterflies. Perhaps the way that benevolence unfolds in our lives is a way we would not be able to look forward to.

However that may be, I was made mellow and serene by the promise within the silence of Kanjirô's house. I noticed the cynical urge to disavow the legitimacy of such feelings on account of the fact they had arisen in a building clearly marked on the tourist's map of Kyôto, but I have grown old enough to recognise such urges as specious.

As I was leaving the building, however, I found this serenity giving way to unease. I was not sure why this was. It could have been because I had been tempted to buy a number of souvenirs, but given up on all but a few postcards after checking how much cash I had left. That is, the weighing of my actions for stinginess and for practicality might have depressed me on one or both counts. I might have been depressed at the thought I was being stingy—even towards myself— with my money. I might also have been depressed by the thought that it was only sensible to be stingy because, even as it was, I had probably overspent this week.

Perhaps more obscurely, after taking many photographs in the house, I saw a sign, by the reception counter, instructing those who wished to take photos to ask for permission, which I had not done. This, too, might have depressed me. In fact, all of these things did, I think, and maybe other things did, too.

Anyway, I left under the shadow of this subtle unease.

It was three in the afternoon and I hadn't eaten lunch. I went in search of a cheap café where I could order something light and perhaps write a little. I walked back up to Gojôzaka and crossed the road to enter Higashiôji-dôri. Across the road again was a "matcha café", which I knew I had passed many times in my life, thinking, "One day, perhaps I'll go in there." I almost passed it by again, especially after looking at a somewhat uninviting menu on which the only items that attracted me cost more than I wanted to spend. But, after walking a little way up the street to look for an alternative, I turned back and went in. I was immediately disappointed. I am not even sure why. I expected the interior to be elegant in some way, but I was struck—without making any deep analysis—by a sense that it was tacky, charmless and pretentious. While a couple in front of me at the counter made their order, I had time and opportunity to escape. I almost did so, but changed my mind. Anyway, I had to eat somewhere, and here I was.

The cold, green-tea soba was tasteless and quickly gone. The matcha *au lait* was somewhat better, though I had felt pressured into ordering a drink. Well, it was over, and I left. Now that I had dealt with the needs of my stomach, I could wander freely until the time came to take transport back to our lodgings.

Walking north along Higashiôji-dôri, I began to feel something of the refreshing freedom of the traveller. This was overlaid, in my case, with memories and with feelings accumulated through a long relationship with Japan. I remembered living in Kyôto some thirteen years ago and walking along this same street. My hopes had then been more excited, my ability to console myself—or perhaps to resign myself—less developed. Looking at the ugly streets of central Kyôto, built for commerce and convenience, not for beauty or mystery, a mere patchwork of greys, I had felt a wind of desolation blow through me. The country for which I had studied hard and travelled far, and of which I had long dreamed, no longer existed, and, what was worse, had been voluntarily dismantled from within by its native souls—the only ones who could ever ensure its survival. The death of a country more surely represents the death of the soul than any individual death. In this world, though the individual dies, he or she may have spiritual existence in the spiritual medium of culture, but if culture itself dies, all we can do is hope there is another world apart from this.

I remembered the anguish of those days—the bitterness of my early disappointments. Even in my joys—or let us say, my fascinations—I had been alone, and so the very sources of consolation renewed my anguish since there had been no one with whom to share them. Now things were a little different. This time, I had not come to Japan alone. This time, also, I benefitted from years of training myself to find beauty wherever I might find myself—silent, lonely training begun, I think, in Japan itself, because of my first disappointments. Again, this time, I also benefitted from experience, wider reading, perhaps even—the thought sometimes troubles me—the ebbing of passion that so often accompanies age. I was able, therefore, to walk along Higashiôji-dôri and feel, for the most part, mellow, pleasant emotions. I cast an eye over ceramics in shop windows, knowing I had no call to buy them — they would clutter my dank, Bexleyheath flat. I stopped outside a Dutch shop selling fashionable clothes and laughed to myself at the shop-window declaration listing "rebelliousness" among their strengths. What are they rebelling against? I wondered. I suspected they did not know. Yes, in short, I was older.

Even so, I caught the bitterness of my younger self on the wind of memory. The roar of traffic and the crowds and constant motion struck me as vulgar, like people who trample oblivious over graves to find a place for their picnic. Why not exercise my traveller's freedom, I thought, and turn up one of these Higashiyama side-streets? I had seen a sign for Tôfukuji and this also prompted me. So I turned, and walked up the rising street. As with sudden shelter from a wind in the lee of a hill, I was relieved at the stillness that once again greeted me here. There were signs of life, but they were a pleasing activity as if held in an outspread palm of peace. A uniformed delivery man on a moped took a package to be signed for. A mother descended the steps from a hidden temple with her tiny daughter.

At the top of these steps was the purple banner, like a curtain, under which they had emerged, and I thought this might indicate the way to Tôfukuji. After climbing the steps, I looked back at the way I had come and the calming glimpse it gave of a network of alleys, like a scene-setting picture for an unremarkable story that is, nonetheless, so gently engrossing as to make one forget oneself.

Then I turned and advanced to what I thought was Tôfukuji. Multi-coloured bunting with a Buddhist tinge to it garlanded, neatly, a temple turret, but I could not see a way in. The alley appeared to be a dead end. To my left, doors were open to tatami-matted rooms, but writing on makeshift signs seemed to indicate, although this was attached to the temple, that it was a restaurant. Moreover, I didn't see "Tôfukuji" written anywhere. Someone looked out at me from the steaming kitchen of the otherwise deserted restaurant. I didn't want to eat now, so I turned around and retraced my steps, a little confused.

An alley went off to what was now my right and, rather than return to the main street, I took this, expecting nothing but vaguely enjoying what had become an aimless wander. I emerged from this alley into another, this one sloping parallel to the alley I had first entered from the main street. There were more people here—Japanese and foreigners—and on either side the way was lined with small but lively-looking cafés, gift shops and so on.

I looked to my right, in the direction in which the slope rose, and saw there what seemed, in some way, to account for the greater numbers here. For a moment I was amazed—a rare happening. Some ascended as if on pilgrimage and some descended as if their pilgrimage was over. Mushrooming above all else with outspread wooden gills, like a monster in an old film, superimposed on a city for which it is too big, uncontainable and therefore unreal, was a temple—I did not know which.

The thought crossed my mind that, though this was a veritable apparition, it was, in fact, the main street, from which I had diverged, that was unreal. This tower filling the view between the alley buildings was careless of both fame and obscurity, pursuing nothing, therefore timeless. The main street, in pursuit of all the things made first famous then obscure by time, would disappear, like something turned inside out and into nothing. I almost thought that those who first built the tower foresaw this. I almost thought they had known the future—they, more than those in pursuit of the future. I wondered when people had lost this insight and forfeited the power to create things that last.

I walked up the slope, since the pagoda brimmed over with significance and I wished to assimilate that significance in some way, to attain a consummation that would convert mere vision into experience. Instinct told me to go closer. From the moment I had seen the pagoda, the question of its name had been in abeyance. I had assumed it was Tôfukuji, but this assumption had been banished from my mind by the presence of the structure itself—although, I feel it was more than a structure, and I struggle to find an appropriate word. The physical structure was as if pickled—saturated in the ideal form whose core it solidified but which it could not entirely soak up. It was a nameless manifestation for me until I drew close enough to see a signboard on the surrounding wooden fence. It was then that I became aware, once more, of the question of the temple's name, and, remembering this question, became aware of myself, too, as a tourist.

It was not Tôfukuji. It was Hôkanji. I have always thought of the names of temples as a sort of lofty gibberish, but I was distinctly aware of something appropriate and meaningful about this name. It was written as "law", "see" and "temple" — The Temple of Law-Seeing. As I write this I have an explanation of the name that satisfies me, though I am not sure I can articulate it. If those first builders of the temple were able to see the future, as I imagined, it was because they knew the law. If, since then, the world has lost sight of the future in pursuit of the future, it is because it has first lost sight of the law. 'The law' is that jewel of which both faith and reason are facets. It was the law that I recognised — that I saw — when I stepped from the previous alley into this.

I read on the signboard how Hôkanji was one of the two or three — I don't remember — outstanding five-storey pagodas still remaining in Japan. In a reliquary are kept some bones said to belong to the Buddha.

I was troubled, though, by the returning consciousness of tourism. What did that consciousness mean? That my experiences were not authentic because I had come for the sake of travel? That my feelings about the place were not valid because I didn't live here? Such thoughts are losing their power over me. Hôkanji withstood, on my behalf, even the charge of tourism laid against me by myself. On top of that, I was not a simple tourist. I had lived and studied in Kyôto for a year and a half. There was a peculiar poignancy in being a tourist where I had once lived. And this reminded me, in turn, that we are all, in some sense, tourists on the Earth. As I feel in Kyôto, both that I belong and that I am forever exiled, so we feel about the world. On the one hand, we have lived here; on the other, all our time here passes as tracelessly as my return to Kyôto, on holiday. As Bashô says, the months and days are eternal travellers.

So, had I succeeded in converting my vision into experience? Do we ever succeed?

Let us say that I succeeded, that what I have written here is the evidence of my success—even so, what can I do with that experience? I can write this, yes. And you can read it. But what can you do with the fact of having read it? Perhaps you will think of something, but the question is only ever pushed back one place further. In the end, what can you do with having done all the things you can do with things you've done? Accept that you are a tourist, perhaps.

The moments disappear in a constant stream. To be the stream is therefore to disappear; to disappear is to be one with the truth; to be one with the truth is to last forever. To last forever is not to disappear; not to disappear is not to be the stream; not to be the stream is to diverge from truth; to diverge from truth is to disappear. To disappear is to be one with the stream . . .

I thought I wanted to disappear. Why? To succeed? Perhaps I want something I can hold forever. Perhaps I will get it.

The Robot

On the 8th of November, a Sunday, we left a rainy Kyôto behind us. We stopped in Nagoya and had lunch with my niece in a restaurant on the top floor of the building above the train station. Then, as darkness fell, we sped on to Nagano, arriving at some time after nine o'clock.

We were staying there at a ryokan — or inn — called Shimizuya. In fact, there were two Shimizuya ryokan in Nagano, and our first taxi took us to the wrong one. Since the first — where we had no reservation — was in a good location and was clean and attractive, it was quite possible we would be disappointed with the second, at which our reservation had been made, and I was even afraid this would be the case. However, though the location was perhaps not as good, we were greeted with natural cordiality on our arrival and shown to a room that immediately gained Bee-chan's approval, and mine. In short, we soon forgot about the first Shimizuya as it disappeared below the horizon of our past into the zone of might-have-beens.

In the tea ceremony and in professions that pre-serve traditional Japanese forms of hospitality, there is a correct way of entering a room and a correct way of opening and closing a shôji. In English, we would call it ritualistic. On the threshold of the room to which we now had the key, the Middle Room (Naka no Ma), as it was called, I could not help thinking about this.

A ritual is a way of framing something, and it is natural that edges are therefore important in ritual, and, with them, entrances and exits. I noticed the lit-eral frame, the literal edge, to the room that for two days would be ours. There was the wooden threshold in which was cut the groove for the shôji and pressed neatly against this threshold was the tatamiberi, that is the material binding the edges of the tatami mats. In this case the tatamiberi was navy blue with patterns in white, black and straw-yellow, the patterns having a diamond motif, single and in overlapping pairs, on backgrounds of threaded pointillist cloud.

I took a photograph—a standing, overhead view— of the slippers provided by the ryokan hanging just over the edge of the wooden threshold so that their toes visually broke the line of the tatamiberi. Precisely this threshold and this tatamiberi seemed to me to embody the experience of some essential quality I am always seeking in Japan.

Affordable to us, the room was no doubt far from the high end of what might be available in terms of traditional accommodation in Japan. The flowers in the vase were a little dry; the scroll in the alcove was faded. But the aesthetics of the tea ceremony teach us to admire precisely this: things of humble appearance, worn by daily usage. "Are we to admire the moon only when it is full, the blossoms only at their height?" Kenkô Hôshi asked this question almost seven hundred years ago. If it had not been already, his resistance to the aesthetic of obvious splendour became Japanese orthodoxy.

Imperfection lent our room pathos, but served to set off what was otherwise neat, fresh and brisk, the way, in a sumi-e painting, the slanting lines of bamboo stalks are made truly elegant by the knots of their joints.

Other details in this elegance were duly noted as we explored. The two futons were in curiously folded heaps on the floor so that merely tugging the pillow ends unfolded them into perfectly made beds. Yukata, towels and so on were prepared for us in a wicker tray. The belts of the yukata were ingeniously folded so that they made compact pentagons. Sliding back another shôji revealed a strange little chamber, no larger than a cupboard, from which was visible a small courtyard where a pine tree grew. I think Bee-chan was even more pleased than I was. It had been her suggestion, when we were planning the trip, to stay in a ryokan at some point, whether it was strictly necessary or not, and this room appeared to be exactly what she had had in mind.

Looking back, it seems to me that, more than with the room itself, I was pleased that Bee-chan was pleased. I was quietly glad that there was no need for us to be ironical or ashamed about enjoying Japaneseness while in Japan. I had even been a little surprised — so accustomed am I to irony in my peers — when Bee-chan had said, for instance, how much she liked autumn-leaf patterns on kimono.

Autumn leaves, in fact, had been something we had both hoped to see in Japan—'kôyô', as the fresh red leaves, usually of the Japanese maple, are called. We had even timed our visit partly with that criterion in mind. We were gradually to discover that our research had been inadequate. We might, in fact, have relied only on my vague memories of living in and visiting Japan before. The cherry blossoms in spring, generally, start from the south, where the warmer temperatures develop sooner, and sweep in a kind of metachronal wave of ephemeral poetry northward. The calm red and yellow fire of the kôyô does the opposite in autumn, sweeping with the colder seasonal atmosphere from the north southward. Therefore the timing of the kôyô depended, of course, on where you might be.

When we arrived in Kyôto, we found the leaves just beginning to gain their autumn tints in patches of beautiful contagion. In particular, we found red and yellow leaves in the garden of the house of silent-film actor Okochi Danjirô and in the grounds of Eikandô Temple, but were aware that, even in these places, the kôyô had not attained the blaze of its full magnificence. When we enquired, we were told that it was still just a little early for kôyô, certainly in Kyôto. Ôhara, just outside Kyôto, was the place to go—so we were advised. But in the end, we did not have time for an expedition to Ôhara.

On the 5th of November, a Dutch lady who sat in front of us on a bus told us she had just come from Nagano and that the kôyô was past its peak there. As Nagano was our first major stop after Kyôto we were afraid that, as we travelled north, we would miss the kôyô in its southward sweep, and, in fact, we never really found the ideal conditions to enjoy a vista of yellow and red leaves, though there were some autumnal trees either side of Nagano's main street.

I had to remind myself of Kenkô Hôshi's words and apply them to kôyô. Wasn't it very Japanese, after all, in its quiet pathos, to just miss the zenith of that red-and-yellow blaze? I consoled myself that it was.

In any case, though we had not had the chance to harvest a vista of kôyô for the storehouse of memory, we had our washiki room in Shimizuya Ryokan, and this looked set to provide us with an aesthetic experience of being in Japan curiously similar to the outdoor experience of gazing at colourful leaves.

When we had settled into the Middle Room a little, I enquired at the reception desk about breakfast. I was told, at first, that breakfast was not included and returned to the room with this news. Later, however, there was a knock on the door. An accommodation had been made for us; there would be breakfast.

We slept late. The dilemma of tourism is that it is at once supposed to be rest and activity. This dilemma was highlighted for us by the fact that so many of Japan's native attractions would close their doors, or lock their gates, somewhere around four or five o'clock, so that if we actually rested, for instance, by sleeping in, we would thereby forfeit many rare opportunities. In our case, in Nagano, what we forfeited in this way was a daytrip to the nearby onsen resort in the mountains, famous for the monkeys that, at a certain time of year, will approach the outside baths and join the human bathers in the hot water. We were, anyway, too early for the monkeys. As the landlord iterated and once reiterated to me with noticeable humour at the edge of his mouth and a humane, everyman twinkle to his eye, it was the "season of love" (*"rabu no kikan"*) for the monkeys, and they had, therefore, no especial enticement to leave the trees of the higher mountain slopes.

Breakfast, at least, was, if I might style it such, cherries in full bloom, an unclouded moon. If I recall correctly, for a price roughly equivalent to £8 each, we were served something that made a full English breakfast appear mere barbarism. Each breakfast was a flotilla of dishes served on small attractive pieces of ceramic and in lacquered bowls. On a long dish roughly the shape of a sectioned and flattened joint of bamboo, a portion of poached salmon sat next to seaweed in soy sauce and sesame seeds and two slices of pink tsukemono. On a round dish was salad and omelette. A lacquer bowl contained lotus roots, mushrooms and so on. There was even a folded paper crane, with each breakfast, placed atop the upturned bowl for soup. To my left and Bee-chan's right, windows showed the small courtyard, with a pine, at the ryokan's centre. Sitting there in my yukata, sampling the breakfast first with my eyes, then with my chopsticks, dish by dish, I felt a sense of satisfaction and the fullness of existence.

Since it was too late, anyway, for an excursion to a monkey onsen (or too early for the monkeys), there was nothing to do after breakfast but explore the overcast and out-of-season Nagano at leisure.

Dressed and ready, we left the ryokan, turning left down the slope, noticing—to my chagrin—that the Taiwanese tea shop on the other side of the road was closed. We were continuing towards the road that would take us to Zenkôji's main gate when Bee-chan exclaimed at something that I hadn't seen. Brought up short in surprise, I looked around and at last saw what had caught her attention. On the opposite side of the road, the side on which the tea shop had been, fully visible through the windows in the wooden doors of the building's façade, was a bearded middle-aged man standing face to face with a robot, its eyes shining and its sleek body as glossy as a new car. (I say "face to face", but the robot came to the height of the man's chest, so that he had to look down at it.)

This was the first time in my life I had seen a robot. Perhaps I should qualify that statement. It is possible, perhaps even probable, that I have seen robots before, depending upon the definition. I realise I don't know precisely what distinguishes 'robot' from 'machine', since machines can run automatically, too. Also, if I say that I have seen toy robots before, this suggests that the robot I saw in Nagano was not a toy. Perhaps you could call it a toy. I'm not sure what its function was—or functions were—other than to be a novelty. So, what I mean by 'robot' in this case must be something like, 'large, sophisticated, anthropomorphic machine'. Anyway, I was distinctly struck, at that moment, that this was the first time I was seeing something, and, more than that, that what I was seeing was something whose existence altered the nature of reality. I was familiar with these objects from science fiction. That I was seeing one now naturally suggested that this world and the world of science fiction had merged. Despite the presence of the word 'science' in the phrase, 'science fiction' suggests, to me, a distinct reality, like that of mythology, so in a sense it was as if I were seeing a centaur for the first time. Of course, the comparison is inexact, but that I felt the existence of the robot to indicate an entirely new reality is true.

The shock lasted a fraction of a second. It is strange, in fact, how quickly the mind can accommodate new realities. What I next felt was a childlike excitement. I forgot, for a moment, adult inhibitions. Perhaps I waved. I think I did. Certainly, the man saw us. He had perhaps been testing his communication with his robot, giving experimental commands, pressing buttons, adjusting settings, and the robot had jolted and swivelled and flashed its lights in that jerky-smooth way familiar to us now from the dance routines of thousands of body poppers, but at some point we had managed to draw his attention away from the stimulating intercourse of man and robot and now he—the man—looked at us with a smile on his face and his head tilted to one side. I took his expression for invitation at first, or something like the smile on the face of a man walking a puppy in the park when someone bends down to pet the animal and asks if it's a boy or a girl. In my head, the existence of the robot had given all humans licence to talk to each other with convivial familiarity. I thought I could cross the road and slide open his front door and say, "Is this your robot? Is he friendly? What words does he know?" and so on, perhaps progressing rapidly to such questions as, "Do you feel your status as a sentient being has changed in proximity to the robot? Does he show signs of independent thought? Do you get nervous that you will wake up with his fingers around your neck? Have you ever caught him in the middle of strange conference with the vacuum cleaner, or mind-melding with the furniture?"

But the man seemed not quite to understand what was obvious to me—that we fellow humans must discuss this robot immediately—and what had at first seemed an invitation in his expression now seemed a question, as if he were asking me to repeat something that had been unclear.

Then I heard Bee-chan talking next to me.

"Come on," she said. "We might be disturbing him."

I considered this, at first skeptically, since the man had been smiling, then because, anyway, I didn't really know how to approach the man and assented to Bee-chan's suggestion that we walk on, I replayed his expression and thought that, after all, it fitted with someone grinning uneasily at an unwelcome stranger and shaking his head.

Anyway, so that was my first robot, I thought, and: that wasn't so bad, after all. It seemed to me that now I had seen a robot, seen how trivial and toy-like they are, they could no longer threaten to convert the waking world into nightmare. The world was itself again—that same old mixture of assumed everyday sanity and peripheral anxieties about time and the cold, contingent shifting of events, sometimes bringing calamity, but please, God, not for me, not yet, and preferably never. The robot peril, at least, was struck from the list of menaces to the human race in general and me in particular. Perhaps most—or all?—of our fears are like this. I was relieved. My tread upon the surface of the Earth felt lighter.

But then a different note began to infiltrate my thoughts. We had turned away from the building where the robot was (another ryokan, as I learnt later) in the direction of the town centre. My thoughts, therefore, also turned back to the Japan we were in search of—the Japan of autumn leaves and tatami mats. It suddenly occurred to me that autumn leaves and robots are aesthetically immiscible, as oil and water are physically immiscible. Robots, I realised, are a menace, after all—an aesthetic menace. I thought about the kind of autumn-leaf pattern that Bee-chan was so fond of, and in my mind I surrounded the robot we had just seen with a decorative frame of such leaves. I could not make them stay there. The robot acted on them as an irresistible repellent. They were pushed back, by the presence of the robot, out of the picture in my mind.

I know very well that we live in a world where warnings of an impending Armageddon of the unbeautiful will be laughed at. However, I also see the links between beauty and goodness clearly enough now that I believe my warning will grow in significance as time passes, not diminish, and I am not tempted to overstate my case.

After the Meiji Restoration, when Japan was forced to open up for trade with the West, the Japanese took up the slogan, "Japanese spirit; Western learning" (wakon yôsai). They thought they could import Western goods and technologies while preserving the Japanese culture. They should have known that physical artefacts are carriers of culture, too. How much, really, of that Japanese spirit can be left now, after all the Western learning that has been imported? Again, I realise this will be taken for an archaic concern, even offensive. Somehow we are supposed to celebrate the differences between cultures at the same time as denying they exist (and all the while, celebrating and denying those differences, we are dismantling them). But maybe it will even be that recent concern, ecology, that returns us to what we have come to consider archaic and offensive.

Some lines from the brush of Nagai Kafû drift back to me on the winds of memory:

"The future has no road to proceed from but that of the past. The morals of a nation are in danger when the people forget the soil and the seasons."

What does a robot know of seasons? It is switched on or off, that is all. Those who desire the utopia of robotics propose to build a world of eternal summer. For them there must only be a full moon and unfalling blossoms. They know nothing of the waning moon, of falling blossoms. They know nothing of autumn.

As for me, autumn is my home, and I am autumn's patriot, never to be reconstructed. I will fall with the red and yellow flag of the falling leaves.

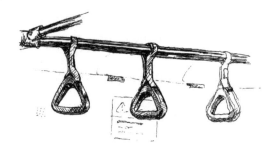

Local Trains and Place Names

Some time after we had returned to England, Bee-chan told me, prompted, it seemed, by nothing in particular, how much she had enjoyed Obusé. She was not sure quite why. It was a quiet little town and we had only spent a couple of hours there, but somehow the atmosphere had pleased her at the time and had remained with her. All this agreed entirely with my own feelings.

I would like to be able to say exactly what it was that made Obusé so appealing, or perhaps I enjoy especially the fact that the appeal comes before and is finally beyond words; either way, I am afraid that I can, with words, only skirt the matter and never will say something definitive. Still, if skirting is all that is available to me, then I shall skirt to the best of my abilities.

While writing notes for this essay, afraid that I had left things too long and wanting something against which to check and with which to compare my recollections, I wrote and asked Bee-chan what she remembered of the place. She sent me back an SMS as follows:

Obusé was quiet and autumnal. Red leaves. Long straight streets with mountains beyond. Crossing over the railway tracks at ground level, not with a bridge— little steps up to the platform. Children and teenagers in white shirts coming home from school. I wondered what it would be like to live there. The shop selling chestnut goods; you bought some gifts and we sat in the window for a while. I posted a postcard in a box by the train station. The pastel chrysanthemum display. I sat on some kind of playground animal nearby. Possibly a smell of woodsmoke, but that may be imaginary. It was one of my favourite parts of the trip.

This is stream-of-consciousness rather than a chronological account, but I am not sure I can give a more evocative summary and I feel that to some extent what I will now write about the place must be redundant. Yet I cannot stop myself. Why? "Possibly a smell of woodsmoke, but that may be imaginary." If there had not been such a scent on the air of that town on that day, then there should have been. I have wracked my memory for anything that might allow certainty on this question, but nothing has. Not in either direction. It should have been; I can imagine that it was; I am on the brink of believing I truly remember—I get no further. Perhaps all cherished memories have their own woodsmoke in this way. And so I must write my account, even if it is redundant, for the sake of the smell of woodsmoke in my head, and also because I know that there are themes I must first outline before developing, and I can best accomplish such an outline through writing about Obusé.

We took the Snow Monkey Express, if I remember correctly. Indeed, there were markings on the station platform indicating where the doors of the various carriages of that train would line up when the train came to a halt. There was a long billboard along the edge of the station track, or else a kind of canvas banner hung from a fence, and this depicted, in primary colours and appealing cartoon images, the attractions of the town. I remember, in particular, autumn leaves and kappa—the water sprites of Japanese folklore. In other words, the billboard was a kind of dream. Who commissioned the image and who created it, I don't know. On the one hand these are interesting questions and on the other, it is interesting that we experience the end result as a pure happening, anonymous, of the group, of the world itself. This was Obusé dreaming— seeming with such a large and colourful image to anticipate large numbers of visitors. But where were those visitors? The place was quiet in the flat of the valley that ended in the mountains visible in the distance. We were the visitors, and the billboard might have been only dreaming, but it was dreaming for Obusé and for us.[1]

---

1 My description of the billboard at the edge of the railway track is wildly inaccurate. In the first draft of this essay, I relied entirely on my memory, which it appears was defective. An examination of the photographs I took in Obusé showed that there were a number of small billboards or posters along the fencing at the

Perhaps I should note here what had brought us to this place. It was simple enough. When we were planning our tour of Japan, we had leafed through this and that travel guide, and in one of them my eye had fallen upon the name of Obusé, and something had intrigued my eye thereabouts, and I had learnt that there was a Hokusai Museum in the town—*the* Hokusai Museum, perhaps. I suppose I also saw it was an easy trip from Nagano. Many things escape my memory, but something about that page and the name printed there remains. Names are wonderful conjurings. Or, to put it another way, there is something wonderful about the power of the human mind to associate a symbol with a reality or a dream, and with any number of realities and dreams at the same time. When I think of my first acquaintance with the name 'Obusé', for instance, an image comes to mind of an ornate circular Japanese crest, or 'mon'. Was there an illustration of this kind on the same page in the travel guide? Perhaps. But whether there was or not, the swirls of the crest come to mind. The image is flexible, too. It can be the pattern on the skin of a ceremonial drum, or it can turn into a design chased on an ancient gong. And it becomes the O of Obusé. All this might seem to some a trivial play of meaningless ideas, but the fact is that my eye

edge of the track. Only one of them had anything in it corresponding to what I had described, and this was a picture of a kappa. I noticed some rather enigmatic writing at the side of this picture, as follows: "人生幻夢耳". What could it mean? It appeared to be written in kanbun, that is, classical Japanese Chinese. After some investigation, I found that what looked like "ear" at the end actually meant "only". The legend, in its entirety, translates, "Life is but a dream." I decided to keep my erroneous description and append this footnote. The painting of the kappa is the work of the artist Takai Kôzan.

fell on a name on a page and because of this, months later and thousands of miles away, Bee-chan and I stepped from a train onto the station platform of the town bearing that name, where we knew no one and no one was waiting for us. Something about the swirl of that mon, something about the beating of that tas-selled, ceremonial drum, had roused my imagination, something in the crash of the gong that was the name 'Obusé' had seemed like some half-mythical memory. And if all this had not been the case, we would not have gone.

Our tickets on the train journey to Obusé were a lit-tle unusual. In order to help us catch the train about to depart, a number of station staff at Nagano had given us two tickets notifying the office we should pay at the other end. I remember these tickets on a mahogany-coloured tray-table on the train itself. As in Bee-chan's memory, we crossed the tracks themselves, on foot, and climbed up steps to another platform, then, pre-senting these two tickets at the office window, we paid our fares and exited. There was something pleasingly old-fashioned and picturesque in all this.

We didn't have much time. We wanted to see a little of the town, but we had come for the museum. After consulting the map we had obtained from the tourist office in Nagano, we decided on a route. This took us by a little park, full of fallen leaves, and we stopped there for a moment. As we did so, a white, flatbed truck—perhaps a Toyota—began to back into the park, the driver and vehicle having a sent-by-the-council look. In the back of the truck, standing straight with fragile and somehow comical balance, were rows of chrysanthemums. It was the time of year, I recalled, for the chrysanthemum festival across Japan. A long, open-fronted tent was being set up in the park to display the chrysanthemums, which were to be judged for prizes. We lingered in the hope of getting some photos of the driver and a number of others who had turned up to help, going about their chrysanthemum business, but, in the end, I hesitated to interrupt them. Bee-chan sat on a large, colourful hermit crab set in the ground nearby, and I sat on a bench. What are people busy with in the small, dreamy town of Obusé with its kappa and its autumn leaves? Delivering chrysanthemums to the local park. Yes, in the dream-world of small towns, that is precisely the sort of thing with which people should be busy.

If there was the smell of woodsmoke, as mentioned, perhaps we first smelt it here—that faint hint that the everyday world was blurring in overlap with the world of dreams, which perhaps inevitably precedes it or perhaps is thrown up in contrast to it. It is as if the woodsmoke binds the two worlds—forms their interface. When you smell woodsmoke—or imagine you do—in the right place at the right time, the blurring of the two worlds is like the falling of autumn sunset rays mellowly on half-closed eyes. It is by such faint and ineffable intimations that a time-and-place becomes meaningfully mysterious to a person. Faint and ineffable—and yet our feelings about this town appear to have been shared.

The museum was relatively small and somewhat airy and pleasant, as such buildings tend to be in Japan, and the exhibits were of enough interest that I regretted we did not have a little more time, but I have no intention of writing a review. Some of the prints and paintings—such as 'The Amida Waterfall in the Depths of the Kiso Mountains'—stick in my mind, but it might be that what worked most immediately and prolifically on my imagination was a looped film giving a biography of Hokusai. I was especially moved by Hokusai's dedication to what many might see as a worldly and therefore an arbitrary thing—that is, simply, art. In his case, it was the art of printmaking and painting. Having, over the years, known of many, great and small and including myself, who have doubted the value of their art, not just in terms of what they might contribute personally, but as a legitimate path in life generally, I was pleased by the impression that Hokusai had no such doubts. Many ask what art is for, and there is a suggestion here, made explicit by many among the many, that art requires a transcendent mandate. I tend to agree, but am discouraged when some proclaim that it does not have that mandate. Hokusai seemed to reverse the matter entirely. Rather than asking what art was for, he made his life a thing *for art*, and in this reversal I sensed by some obscure but resounding instinct that he had, indeed, grasped the transcendent.

The film mentioned the fact that Hokusai changed his name over thirty times. A couple of these names, such as 'Crazy Old Man Mad on Painting' (画狂老人) testify to the abovementioned dedication. Among the list of names, I especially noticed 'Gunma-Tei' (群馬亭), which translates as something like 'Gunma Pavilion', with 'pavilion' approximating a gazebo or place to rest. What a strange intersection of associations this name was for me. Gunma is the prefecture where I lived when I first went to Japan. I have an idea that the Japanese view it somewhat as Americans view Arkansas, where I have also spent time; at least, the Japanese are as surprised at my going to Gunma as the Americans are at my going to Arkansas. The third ideogram, 'tei' (亭), is one that I encountered more often in Taiwan, where it was used to indicate kiosks and small, roadside shops and stalls. So, altogether, the name conjured up for me a Chinese-style tea-kiosk, with a large parasol over a table nearby, perhaps, at a roadside stop somewhere out of the way in Gunma. I have been to similar places, and simply seeing the name, I was seized with an almost intolerable and yet wonderfully sweet yearning to go to such a place again, indeed, even to *be* such a place, as Hokusai seemed to declare himself to be such a place by adopting the name.

If the above example has shown the reader that names are wonderfully powerful things for invoking all kinds of spirits—but especially those of time and place—then half my purpose in writing this essay is accomplished. However, this is such an attractive theme for me that I would like to elaborate on it, at least a little. It is a theme that cries out for examples. What's more, as it is a theme that occurred to me—by no means for the first time—in Obusé, to which we had been taken by a picturesque train that our Japan Rail Pass did not cover, and as we noticed the idiosyncrasies of the little station at which we alighted, and these somehow framed our time in Obusé, I would suggest that the theme of the evocative power of names very much intersects with trains and train stations, and so I hope to treat that intersection, too.

But first, let us take leave of Obusé in its golden November. Obusé, the home from home of Hokusai's final years, town of fallen leaves and chestnuts.

When we exited the museum, we saw a shop selling all manner of chestnut-themed confectionary and decided to have a look, with the possibility in mind of buying gifts either for those who we were still to visit in Japan, or for people back home. It was the kind of shop that you might imagine to do well on Oxford Street in London, but which is mysteriously common in small and medium-sized towns in Japan — well-staffed, the assistants wearing immaculate shop uniforms and providing service of eerie efficiency, the premises (rather than quaintly dilapidated as they might be in Britain) bright, clean, spacious and airy. The glazing of the shop seemed almost entirely to take up three walls, letting in all the mellow sunshine of the autumn day. The assistants, always pleasantly bustling, never listless, allowed us to sample this or that little cake or biscuit, and, indeed, we made some purchases, perfectly wrapped for us in the usual pastel-patterned paper of Japanese shops. Sitting on the padded seat at the window, we ate chestnut tarts — a sample of the local specialty. And the window provided a sample for us, too, of place and time, for the sake of what some hold cheap and others know to be priceless — experience, and what experience becomes, which is, and only can be, memory. At least while we remain in the realm of time.

On our way back to the station, the streets were lively with gangs of white-shirted schoolchildren, perhaps on their way home or perhaps merely gathering to cross roads as if this itself were the most natural activity of such gaggles. The fresh chatter of their presence, their immersion in their own routine of life with only a cheerful, sidelong acknowledgement of our brief intersection with it, formed the perfect human foreground to the serene autumn skies at the end of the straight, quiet streets. The serenity is constantly alive with these voices, the contrast seemed to say, as if intending by this that we should carry some wordless understanding, between chatter and sky, away with us.

Aware of the time, hurrying, we arrived at the train station. In a little red postbox by the station entrance, Bee-chan posted a postcard, as if we were clocking off.

Farewell, Obusé! Who knows when or if we shall ever meet again?

Soon we were on a train to Sendai.

Now, let us set aside chronology for a while and concentrate on theme. I remember, at some time during my many visits to Japan, waiting for a train at Yamamaé Station in Gunma Prefecture, having just parted company with a family in Gunma to whom I am connected. Yamamaé is a little country station of the kind I like. It is not especially distinguished in any way that I can define, except, somehow, in my own sentiments. Standing there, on the platform, I took a photograph of the sign with the station name on it— something I am inclined to do on occasion, as if the written name is the place itself—and felt something of the pathos of the traveller as evoked in the titles of the *Otoko wa Tsurai yo!* film series. There is a word in Japanese, 'tabigokoro', literally 'journey heart', which indicates the desire to embark on a journey. Travel writing has a distinguished place in Japanese literature, too. Is this odd for an archipelago of Japan's size, which for hundreds of years shut itself off from intercourse with the outer world? I don't know, but it is true that I feel strangely sentimental about travel while I am in Japan. It is such feelings that prompt me to take photographs of the station name on a signboard, for instance. If I were the accomplished linguist I would like to be, I would know whether there existed in any other language a travel-related word as romantic as the Japanese 'kusamakura', or 'grass pillow', once an actual object woven by travellers, now indicating the act of sleeping in the open on a journey. Since I am not such a linguist, I will for the time being believe there is none. And place names are often glorified in classical Japanese literature with 'makura-kotoba' — 'pillow words' — that act somewhat like Greek epithets, so that "*tama-shiki no miyako*", for instance, in Kamo no Chômei's *Hôjôki* is, "the jewel-strewn capital", and near the beginning of Ueda Akinari's 'Shiraminé' ('White Peak'), "*ashi ga chiru Naniwa*" is "Naniwa of the scattering reeds". The effect is that the place name itself becomes a poetic ritual, echoing and re-echoing in hundreds of literary references. Those places have all changed since anyone wrote in the classical style, and they were changing, too, before the modern period, as the poets often lamented. *There is moss on the eaves of the palace! The great days have passed!* So we cannot revisit those places whose names echo eternally in poetry, or not as they were. Yet the echoes of the names, with their makura-kotoba in their train, like the kappa on the billboard of Obusé, remain in the dreams of the place, surely. The celebration of the names has gifted the world with ghosts, so that I will always wonder what it was like to visit the purple-scented plains of Musashino[1] as the poets knew (or perhaps only dreamt) of them.

But I am in danger of straying . . . Yes, the constant danger of tabigokoro. Let me return, anyway, to the little station, Yamamaé, and the sign of which I have taken a photograph more than once. What does the name mean? 'Yama' is 'mountain' and 'maé' is a common component of place names, simply meaning 'in front of'. So: In Front of the Mountain. It is really a plain and simple name, but that's what charms me. It is not always the bizarre and the eccentric that are evocative.

So, from Obusé it was to Sendai that we went, and Sendai we intended as the metropolitan base from which we might explore, a little, the Miyagi countryside. In particular, we wanted to visit an onsen resort. There were, I believe, three candidates for this, but in the end—I can't recall exactly why—we settled on Naruko. There must have been some particular reason, because in at least one sense it was not very convenient. It was quite far away, and we did not intend to stop overnight. It required a change of train at Furukawa to get there, and the town lay almost in the northernmost tip of the prefecture. Indeed, it is the farthest north I have yet been in the Japanese archipelago. The town that was distinguished, for me, by this superlative— the farthest north—was a small town, its streets steep with the slope of the mountain on which it was built, and an obscure town, though, as one often finds out

---

1 ". . . *murasaki niou Musashino no hara*". I know that 'murasaki' here means the flower *lithospermum purpurocaeruleum* and 'niou' means 'bloom' rather than 'give off fragrance', but I have translated with poetic licence.

on discovering such towns, in some way an 'historical' settlement that was once significant, for instance as a stopping station on a trade route or the place of retirement for some noted feudal lord, or the main supplier of silk or some other raw material to the rest of the country. In the case of Naruko, it is one of the places mentioned by Bashô in his *Narrow Road to the Deep North*.

南部道遥に見やりて、岩手の里に泊る。

小黒崎・みづの小嶋を過て、なるごの湯より尿前（しとまえ）の関にかかりて、出羽の国に超えんとす。

この路旅人稀なる所なれば、関守にあやしめられて、漸として関をこす。

大山をのぼつて日すでに暮ければ、封人の家を見かけて舎を求む。

三日風雨あれて、よしなき山中に逗留す。

We gazed awhile along the road that stretched north, and found lodging that night in the village of Iwadé. We passed Ogurosaki and Mizunokojima, and departing the hot springs of Narugo,[1] we journeyed towards the Shitomaé Barrier, hoping to cross over into Dewa Province.

In this region few travelled the roads, and the guards at the pass looked upon us with suspicion; it was narrowly we made it through.

---

1 This, presumably, is Naruko. I notice some of the other names also altered a little in pronunciation.

By the time we had climbed the great mountain, the sun had sunk and we sought shelter in the house of a mountain guard.

For three days wind roared and rain lashed, and we had no choice but to remain in the mountains.

And it was at this pass that Bashô wrote the following haiku:

蚤虱 馬の尿する 枕もと

Fleas! Lice!
And a horse empties its bladder
By my pillow.

Incidentally, the 'shito' in 'Shitomaé' is written with the ideogram for 'urine'.

As for us, when we arrived at Naruko, we found beyond the station a quiet and attractive huddle of buildings, mainly with the look of gift shops, small, dimly lit eateries and the like, so that there was not an immediate sense of a local population apart from those catering to tourists visiting for the bath houses. Indeed, near the very top of the steep road, before the slope became dark and wooded, there rose a modern, multi-storey hotel that seemed ludicrously out of place. We stood outside, so that the glass doors sensed our presence and slid automatically open. There was a receptionist in a green uniform at the desk, but there was not a sign of guests. It seemed likely that one building could have housed more than the population of the town itself, at least as it was visible to us. But the road on which the hotel stood was full of the smell of sulphur, which tells of authentic—not contrived—hot springs, and a certain chill in the air combined with the archaic gaiety of the awnings of the bath houses somehow staved off disappointment, despite the sense of lack and loneliness and strangeness.

The bathhouse for which we had come was over a century old, with antique timbers in its interior. In fact, there was little by way of the varied amenities of the more modern bathhouses, and there was not even a view. We had come a long way to spend an hour in an old, steamy wooden box with strangers. A drunken old man who said he was a teacher spoke to me for half the time I was there. When we had finished and met again outside the bathhouse, we went and had a meal in a small place where we were the only customers, and we ate in the near-desolate silence of the staff's attentiveness, while the dusty winds of time seemed to moan outside. At one point, Bee-chan's glass shattered into tiny splinters, augmenting the silence and the nervousness of the place even more, and we were ushered to another table while the hazard of broken glass was dealt with by the waitress as if it were a medical emergency. It was an inexpressibly precious evening.

I will not pretend that at the time our enjoyment brimmed and that small dissatisfactions were forgotten. But I have mentioned before that I, for one, have learnt from Japan to be a connoisseur of the dreary, the deficient and the underwhelming, of all that frustrates the straightforward consummation of expected pleasure.

94

And yet, perhaps I am not enough of a connoisseur. As I sit down to write this paragraph, it is midnight on the 26th (or 27th) of October, 2016. I have spent an hour, perhaps closer to two, on Facebook, and when I consider how wholly unproductive that time was, and the strange, unsettled emotions involved, I must conclude that I am still a very lonely person to be susceptible to a social media addiction—an addiction to a bright screen that promises but never delivers meaningful interaction. The dusty wind of time still has much to teach me. I should be able to stand on some street corner of some run-down resort in the mountains at night, alone, with all doors closed to me, and smile at the utter cold obscurity of my fate. To know how indifferently I am forgotten by the world, and how hard is the ground I must tread while I'm alive—this is to meet death. And when I meet death, I wish to be able to shake hands and to smile in the silence of understanding. I wish the dusty, moaning wind of time to be my friend, my familiar spirit, so that its presence, which outwardly is cold, to my inner essence is an infallible warmth. And what then? Well, only that if I can achieve such a thing, if it is possible, I will then come back as a ghost for you, dear reader, whose eye too seldom I meet with mine, and find you when you are on just such a desolate corner, some lonely night, and I shall bring you smiles in the dusty wind of time and the cold of obscurity. Yes, I hope to meet you there.

And so you see why I might attempt to be a connoisseur of such things? It is part of my mission to be a friendly ghost.

But now, to return from this digression, I'm afraid I might, anyway, have done Naruko a slight injustice. For all its deep backwater silence, it retained a peculiar, incomplete charm, a charm as if flitting on its evening air elusively with ragged bat-wings. One concrete particular that typified this charm was the fact that there were warm footbaths, at which you could sit, outside at the train station, the water presumably coming from the same hot-spring source as that for the bathhouses. These footbaths were individually named, conferring on them the distinction of place; a detailed map should mark them by name as geographical features. This raises the question, of course, where a place ends and begins, in time as well as space. I am among those content to believe such a question highlights the mystery of the spirit of place rather than dispels it.

Our last location in Naruko before catching the train back to Furukawa for our connection to Sendai, was the footbath known as Poppo-no-Ashiyu.

Such was Naruko. And what might the name 'Naruko' itself mean? It is formed of two ideograms, the first of them meaning 'cry' and the second, 'child'. So the name of this town is Crying Child? Yes, but not in the sense that you might be imagining. The English word 'cry' designates at least two different things—to weep and to call. The ideogram in this case is used not for 'weep' but for the cry of an animal. So, do we imagine a feral child, perhaps some Japanese counterpart of Romulus and Remus, howling or hooting at the edge of a wood? But wait, both 'weep' and 'call' in Japanese are read as 'naku' and this is 'naru', like . . . the chime of a bell. Chiming Child? Perhaps. I suppose speculation, if investigation turns up nothing, must be wholly idle, but I am glad the world still contains such irregularities for imagination to snag on.

Both Obusé and Naruko are places where we actually went, as, indeed, is Yamamaé, if catching a train at the station counts. However, it is inevitable that there are more fascinating, obscure and evocative place names among the places one hears of but does not visit than there are of places one ends up going to. It is even part of the fabric of travel that one becomes increasingly aware of such names, and of the fact of existence they imply—that, to quote the words of the song, the wonderful, unknown thing you are seeking is "always just around the bend". Sure enough, you'll catch glimpses of it—from a train window, perhaps—but even if you go to Obusé, even if you stay, will you ever live in the Obusé of your dreams? . . . I find I do not wish to give a final answer to that question. Let us just say, it might be just as well, at some point, to cultivate the art of treasuring, too, the names of the places to which you have never been, or which you might only have glimpsed in transit, or where you only spent an accidental hour one night having lost your way.

I don't keep a comprehensive list of such names, but I know them very well whenever I hear or read them. There are one or two of them on the Ryômô Line between Yamamaé and Maébashi. For instance, Omata. In fact, this one intrigues me partly because it's strange without suggesting any immediate, clear images. It becomes a little otherworldly to me for that reason alone, as if the name were a screen to hide a secret life. I think I have seen the name on road signs and gantries, and each time have gone into a half-conscious daydream about it. The 'o' simply means 'little', with, for me, all the attractive connotations of that word. What is little is secret and obscure. But what does the ideogram for 'mata' (俣) mean? It's not an ideogram I have seen anywhere else except in this place name.[1] For this reason, I vaguely thought of it as the kind of character in more common use in China. While writing this essay I decided to free-associate on the ideograms for 'Omata' and see what images they brought to mind before looking up the meaning of 'mata'. This is what I wrote:

> Small, obscure Chinese robots, without technical compatibility with any other electronic systems, work in a factory sorting the parts of slaughtered pigs in buckets. During their breaks they smoke and spit tobacco and play cards with a bloodstained deck.

I suppose it might not sound a very inviting place to visit, but that's one of the dangers of trying to tease these vague, wispy dreams into specific images.

After this exercise, I looked up 'mata'. It appears to mean 'place of parting' or 'boundary'. So, 'Minor Boundary', perhaps? Or did two people part company here centuries ago—an event whose sadness is now forgotten and only obscurely echoed in this name? Again, perhaps I shall never know. Another reminder, in some ways refreshing, that my whole life is

---

1 A little research leads me to believe that Omata Station does not serve the Omata—apparently barely even a hamlet—that I have seen sometimes on road signs, but that it serves, instead, an outlying district of the town Ashikaga.

saturated in the unknown—and with this realisation comes hope: in the unknown is potential for infinite renewal.

As it turned out, when I looked 'mata' up, I saw that the ideogram was the very opposite of what I had supposed. Rather than being one of those characters in more common use in China, it was what the Japanese call a 'kokuji', that is, one of the rare Kanji they have constructed themselves out of Chinese elements. Had it been the former kind of Kanji it would have been rare in the Japanese context, and exotic; as the latter it was probably even rarer, though it was not exotic in the same sense of the word. Strangeness, we might be reminded, comes from within as well as from without.

Another of the stations between Yamamaé and Maébashi on the Ryômô Line—incidentally, the line itself has a place in my heart, as does the Tarka Line in Devon—is Kunisada. This name entered that part of my consciousness where imagination is active many years ago, although my memory of my first encounter with it is uncertain. I suppose I saw that name, too, first as a name on a sign, or in a timetable, or some such thing. I have a memory of finding it immediately striking, as expressing phonetically, in a single unit, a grand and deadly loneliness of the kind I would like to express myself at greater length—in a novel. I did homage to the name, in fact, by giving it to a character in my novella, *Shrike*. Mrs Kunisada, the widow. Japanese readers, however, already have strong associations with the name and might well find my usage jarring. It belongs, for instance, to the ukiyo-e artist, Utagawa Kunisada, to the nineteenth-century gambler,

Kunisada Chûji, and to the baseball player Kunisada Yasuhiro. Can my own daydream associations, as a foreigner, be strong enough to overcome the native spirits of cultural association? It seems unlikely, and yet, surely, a stranger's dream of a place is as interesting in some respects as the dream of the native? Is there a means by which these dreams can meet?

It is one kind of skill to recognise what is evocative for oneself—the primary skill for an artist, since it is the beginning of the development of original intuition—but it is another skill to judge what will be evocative to a broad mix of people. To some extent the latter skill is the result of mere knowledge—one is acquainted with a certain society or culture. But if it is to have lasting effect, surely such a skill must be linked to some understanding of the dreams that humanity shares. I believe this was what T.S. Eliot was indicating with the 'objective correlative'. But is this a skill, or is it simply that we work under the aegis of a particular Muse—one which is able to marshal the local and temporal spirits of Earth and put them to work making sets (for stories, paintings and so on), designing costumes, playing roles, supplying theatrical properties of all kinds for a cosmic production?

Perhaps I am simply too much in the habit of casting myself on the mercy of my personal Muses, who are, artistically, as local deities; I hope they will intercede on my behalf with the universal Muses, the deities of the cosmic order itself. I am afraid I will throw myself on the mercy of those Muses again now. Inspired by timetables, maps and itineraries, I shall list the names of the stations on the two railway lines I have mentioned above, and give commentary on some of them.

The Ryômô Line
Oyama—小山
Omoigawa—思川
Tochigi—栃木
Ôhirashita—大平下
Iwafuné—岩舟
Sano—佐野
Tomita—富田
Ashikaga—足利
Yamamaé—山前
Omata—小俣
Kiryû—桐生
Iwajuku—岩宿
Kunisada—国定
Isesaki—伊勢崎
Komagata—駒形
Maébashi-Ôshima—前橋大島
Maébashi—前橋
Shin-Maébashi—新前橋
Ino—井野
Takasakitonyamachi—高崎問屋町
Takasaki—高崎

The Tarka Line
Barnstaple
Chapelton
Umberleigh
Portsmouth Arms
King's Nympton
Eggesford
Lapford
Morchard Road

Coppleston
Yeoford
Crediton
Newton St. Cyres
Exeter St. Davids
Exeter Central

Listing them all like this, I feel, almost completely, that I do not have to explain their attraction. These are all proper nouns. That is, they take capital letters in English and name unique, unrepeatable features of the world (the name might be repeated, but the feature isn't, just as Paris, Texas is not Paris, France). As such, we can feel more closely in proper nouns something of the seemingly arbitrary particularity of language itself. The world is made of particulars that only shared experience and a name allow us to grasp. A look in the eye or a tone of the voice might be necessary, too. Much of the understanding of literature relies on this—perhaps, indeed, it is this that distinguishes literature from philosophy. Could we explain to an alien why the title of Eric Morecambe's biography, *Life's Not Hollywood, It's Cricklewood*, is funny? Could we explain to this alien why the stage name 'Morecambe' would have been appropriate for this comedian whether he had been born in that place or not? But, let us suppose, as I have said, this realm of particular experience is more the realm of literature than philosophy, nonetheless, philosophy duly recognises it, and calls it the *Lebenswelt*. It is the *Lebenswelt* of language that such lists of names conjure for us—the world in which we live. And since they are all *Lebenswelt*, in some sense what matters more than the individual names is the

102

list itself; we understand these words somehow, and the gaps between them resound with that understanding. It is good that some seem plainer and some more peculiar than others. The plainness of one, the peculiarity of another, and the contrast between them, all are ways of manifesting the underlying knowledge of the *Lebenswelt*, which, paradoxically, is itself not a particular, but a universal.

Omoigawa—An evocative and unusual name in quite a straightforward way, as it seems to mean 'River of Thoughts' (or 'Remembered River'—the permutations are numerous). I imagine gazing, in Omoigawa, from atop a bridge, in autumn, watching yellow leaves float slowly through my own reflection in the dark water below.

Iwafuné—As written in the Roman alphabet, it is the 'f' that catches me here. There is a quirky femininity to this name. I can imagine it as the name of a fifties screen heroine known for playing tragic waitresses or singers luckier in fame than in love. It seems to mean 'Boulder Boat' or 'Boat of Rock'. An interesting object to imagine. How would it float?

Ino—The first thing that comes to my mind is wild boars. This is certainly in part because the Japanese word for 'boar' is 'inoshishi'. But I am tempted to think the wild brevity of the word—two vowels separated by one of the most primitive consonants—also plays its part here. Short words can often have more mystique than long ones. We assume they are older, worn smooth with the passage of centuries. This name means 'Well Field'. So, I picture a boar foraging by an old well in a field.

Eggesford—There's something slightly comical or absurd about this name, as if it indicated a scene in which Humpty Dumpty and various of his kinsfolk were trying to cross a river, but that is only something that has occurred to me at this moment. Almost subliminally, I have always been aware of some humorous oddity about the name, but for me it has, primarily, a romantic ring to it. Whenever I am on the Tarka Line and the train stops at Eggesford Station, and I look out at the cottage-like station building on one side and the level crossing ahead, I seek out, with my eye, the station sign, and thereby obtain some obscure satisfaction, the matter of which is simply that such a place as Eggesford exists and I am once more on a train momentarily stopping there.

Why is Eggesford special to me in this way? I am not sure I would want to give a complete explanation even if I could, but the truth is that even in my own mind the reasons for this are blurry. I believe I have overlapping associations with the place. I believe a friend had some adventure there last century, when we were both teenagers, and that he told me a little of it, and that it had inspired in me a longing for the place. I believe that, thereafter, we would occasionally pronounce the name "Eggesford" fondly and knowingly, with a suggestion that someday—*someday*—we should go there together. I think perhaps that for my friend the place was associated with a now irrecoverable love affair. I even think we strayed upon its outskirts one night, walking in the wooded hills in the small hours, and that I saw blue, peaceful flames upon an uprooted tree struck by lightning—a vivid memory which my friend, who is part of it, never recalls when I mention it to him.

From the above, no doubt you can tell that Eggesford must be a very peculiar and special place indeed. I like to think that if I visit there one day, if, that is, a day arrives when I do not simply look with satisfaction at the station sign while the train stands still to let others on and off—do others ever get on and off?—but by some curious inspiration step from the train to the platform of that country station, I will find that, even in age, as I tread without guidance the ways that lead from the station exit, a steady, peaceful knowing grows in me that I have re-entered childhood, or rather, entered strangely and newly all that in childhood I half-expected in a waking dream, yet missed. After many fields, in broad grounds, where trees are grown with beards of moss unchecked since the time of Eden, I shall see a rambling house, and around it children frolicking in a fête. In short, I shall find that I have come to some such place as the young Meaulnes discovers by accident in the novel by Alain-Fournier, and I shall become a child, in keeping with all that is obvious and unlived in my heart, and never leave again.

And such is Eggesford.

Morchard Road—I was tempted to write of Umberleigh. I was tempted, also, by King's Nympton. Then, suddenly, the mysterious appeal of Morchard Road, until now so invisible to me it was as if the name had never once been impressed on my memory,

105

became apparent. That's the way it works with place names.

Morchard. What, indeed, is a morchard? On the one hand, it sounds like the name of a gallant, well meaning, but perhaps somewhat clumsy young man. Extending his hand to shake yours, he treads on your toe, releasing you, in horror, to catapult you into the flowerbed, then steps back himself in reaction, only to topple your prize-winning vegetable from the display table where it rests. He's rather tall and not exactly slender. He would be good at fisticuffs, if he were not such a spaniel; a wonderful lapdog, if he were not so large; an appealing jester, if only he were quick enough. He intended to propose to his love, Annerleigh, in a hired suit of armour, but the visor clanged down at the wrong moment and cut him short. She was intercepted by the dashing Terenton, who, though a rogue in manners is nonetheless decent in his underlying manliness, and Morchard, unable to hate him, converted his love for Annerleigh to the brotherly, and his rivalry with Terenton to something like the same.

Fanciful, perhaps, but what are these names for otherwise? However, the name of this station is not simply 'Morchard' but 'Morchard Road'. That is, it must be the road where he lives, or, rather, since no road is named after someone who has newly moved in, the road where he once lived and where he became a familiar figure, was known without much celebration as a 'character', his mop of chestnut hair hiding a wayward shoal of unknown thoughts and drifting, at a certain era, regularly, by these bricks, past this shopfront, turning this corner. At some point during this era, without anyone exactly deciding it, he came to stand for the road itself; he was its living ghost.

And he still lives, but not here. He is older, and his dreams are altered, and if some say he is a different person, he might even agree, and then, with a wry smile, joke, "Different to whom?" And yet he has occasion still to visit the old road, which, now both he and road are other than they were, bears his name, and the older residents, on such occasions, will say, "Is that Morchard? I do believe it's Morchard. Look, there goes Morchard." "Morchard?" the younger enquire. "Yes. Morchard of Morchard Road. He's the one the whole road's named after. You live here and you don't know that?"

Morchard, meanwhile, on this visit of mysterious purpose, walks by the same old bricks as before, which now become a wall just low enough for someone of his height to peer over, which he does, knowing what he'll see. Once it was merely a long garden of apple blossoms. Among his memories of this place is a memory of scrumping—himself and two other lads being chased away by a whiskered old man who must have been the gardener. They had truly believed they were in for a thrashing on that occasion, but somehow managed to scrabble over the wall in time and nothing came of the incident. It is hard to know what to think of such memories. They seem untouchable—even by God.

Since then, the orchard, losing its master perhaps, has fallen into neglect, and with the potters field of the nearby church being now closed to new burials, has come to be used also as a graveyard overflow. The old rows of apple trees still stand, with gaps here and there, and between them now are the grey slabs and gravelled oblongs that memorialise human remains, in spring and summer to be covered with blossoms, and in autumn with fallen apples, pecked at by birds and symbolising the fate of those beneath the earth.

Morchard can think of nothing more appropriate than that the soil over which in boyhood he romped and sported, as spirited and self-unknowing as in a dream, should now be full of graves.

What a place it is that so contains the truth of his life! And what to call this strange garden where apples still grow and might be eaten by those who dare, and where human forms and memories decompose? What, if not a 'morchard'?

Crediton—Crediton is the stop just before Exeter, if one does not count the request stop Newton St. Cyres, at which I do not remember the train ever stopping. As such, Crediton feels like a kind of vice-Exeter—Exeter's understudy. It has about it the vaguely comical attraction of the eclipsed. From its very name it sounds as if it is striving for worthy reputation but succeeding only in dreariness.

Many years back, for a period, I visited Crediton regularly for the purposes of a community theatre project. I remember it fondly—the long main street, still, then, grey with a settled age and not resembling the meretricious high streets of today that, like websites reliant on the templates of remote infrastructures, all look the same.

I remember the park. I remember the sense then, in the early nineties, that this provincial green and grey was restfully eternal. I remember the great glass frontage of a pie shop, the façade otherwise painted a stodgy dark green.

For a while afterwards I would always start a little, on the Tarka Line, when the train stopped at Crediton, and feel I should be getting off, though knowing I shouldn't. I wonder if the same likeable Devon girls come of age there now as did then—with long brown hair and black jeans, smoking cigarettes, paired in an almost masculine companionship, listening, perhaps, to Alien Sex Fiend, Half Man Half Biscuit or The Waterboys, always seeming to be skiving off something, more bantery than flirty, and hailing me ever in a rosy-cheeked manner as if I were an established local eccentric and we could, from the start, assume we were friends.

May blessings be heaped forever upon the companionable, scruffy girls of Crediton!

Perhaps it is time to pause. May I suggest that the reader spend some time alone, in a quiet room, or perhaps while taking a leisurely train journey, to examine the above lists of station names and to dream, a little, of what they might mean?

I would like to end this essay with one more list of station names, and some brief commentary.

Chûshojima—中書島
Kangetsukyô—観月橋
Momoyama-minamiguchi—桃山南口
Rokujizô—六地蔵
Kowata—木幡
Ôbaku—黄檗
Mimurodo—三室戸
Uji—宇治

These are the stations on the Keihan Uji Line, a line of strictly local trains (no express services) running between Chûshojima, in Fushimi-ku, Kyôto, and Uji. There is more than one way to get to Uji by train from Kyôto, but if you are taking the Keihan Line, for instance from Sanjô in Kyôto, you change from the main line to the branch line at Chûshojima.

The history of the line might be interesting to some. It seems Keihan were already planning the line by 1910, but the death of Emperor Meiji—the figurehead for Japan's opening to the world and subsequent modernisation—in 1912, precipitated such an influx of mourners to Uji, that the construction of the line was, as it were, fast-tracked, and it was opened for public service in June, 1913.

I took this line with Bee-chan on the 5th of November, 2015. It was one of those rare days in life in which much is done, with a sense of pleasing leisure throughout, even if one must, inevitably, hurry now and then. We had been, again, to Tetsugaku no Michi, the Path of Philosophy, and there I had bought us chestnuts, from a roadside pedlar. I wanted to get us to the tea shops of Uji before they closed, and so we took the Keihan train, a little breathless, perhaps from Demachi-yanagi,

110

or somewhere near its source in the north of Kyôto. When we changed at Chûshojima, a great cloud of undifferentiated memory rose up in me. At the time I had stayed in the Ôbaku dormitory, I had taken this train all the time, and Chûshojima was a fixture of my mental landscape, even if only incidentally.

Our connecting train, once we had boarded, pulled away from the station, and a curious thing happened. As the announcements came on over the P.A. system, telling us the next station, the exact sequence of the names of stations, between this and Uji, came back to me. I had never attempted to learn those names, but their repetition, in the background, day after day, during that fugitive period of my existence, must have left a living imprint on my mind. Few poems can be as poignant and subtle, as phantasmal and haunting to me, as that list of names.

Some of them are more exquisite to me than others:

"Kowata. Kowata."

The prerecorded, high-pitched female voice repeated the name over the speakers as in my head. How inexpressible it was! In some sense, I was brought back to life, though still living. I heard the announcement with something of the same curious delight as a person might who had died and been buried, only to be disinterred again and revivified to all the forever inscrutable details of daily life in which there yet rings some faint, mysterious bell of familiarity—faint, yet in the purity of its vibration penetrating all things.

The untidiness of electric cables above the tracks, the slow swerve of the train alongside houses with futons slung over balconies to air, and the tawdry modern buildings nonetheless retaining the clutter and life that make some ukiyo-e townscapes attractive—as the train took us through this, I remembered the exact mental and emotional texture of those lost days. I had been alone then.

Rokujizô.

Kowata.

All I had done then was without purpose and flowed straight and irretrievably into death, like the sands of an hourglass with its bottom removed.

Ôbaku.

Yes, the stop where I had always got off to go home, where I had made friends with rusting vending machines in alleys. All that time like a flash of sun on the windows of a passing train.

Mimurodo.

No one will ever know, and it was not special except that I lived it. I lived it, and uselessly, wonderfully, through these names and this slow, every-stop-stopping train, it lives again in me.

Uji.

We alighted.

Space Heaters

Having been to Japan I have done what I suppose every person does who spends any significant time in a country of which they have long dreamed; I have lost from my personal map of the world a country—of dreams—and replaced it with another—of experience. The process is not as simple and as absolute as that makes it sound, but sometimes a grief is involved almost as if it were.

In any case, what I want to talk about here is not what I have lost, but what I have gained. At least, I want to give an example. I will only mention briefly the kind of thing that has been lost in order to set off the gain by contrast.

Then again, much of what I have lost is lost so completely that I am not sure I can definitely recall the dream country of Japan that was known to me before I ever knew the real country. To some extent, I simply expected *more* of what is particular to Japan historically and culturally—more spotless houses of paper and wood, more people walking in the streets in kimono of one kind or another, more bamboo groves,

113

more paper lanterns, more people composing haiku beneath cherry blossoms in zen bliss, more ritual disembowelment and so on. Tellingly, even the Japanese focus in literature and other arts on the everyday has led—in its selectiveness—to the production of a conglomerate hyper-reality—an understated simplicity that is extraordinary. In its most abstract terms, it was this hyper-reality of which the dream of Japan was formed, and this which I anticipated. I suppose I believed that every day I would be immersed in a kind of sauna of alien ritual transforming the most trivial of mundane interactions into a drama of austere beauty; I dreamt, you might say, that the entire country would be the stage of a Noh theatre.

I remember—somehow—a fantasy I had early on when I was learning Japanese. I would arrive in the country, still only with rudimentary language skills, and lodge with a family. The cultural barriers would be forbidding, but one day, as the high morning sun shone in through the open paper doors onto the bare floor where I knelt struggling with words, I would get out the complete sentence, "*Mizu wo kudasai,*" ("Water, please.") and the lady of the house would bring me a glass of water, thereby satisfying that most basic of human needs, and for no reason that I dare attempt to explain, we would both laugh and I would understand the soft human warmth beneath the iron mask of Japanese culture, and how the two were, in fact, one, and thus begin my own journey towards wearing such a mask myself, the better to be soft and warm beneath it, in a way that only myself and the Japanese would understand. In this daydream, I even stretched out on the floor, as if prostrating myself before a sacred altar, and giggled with the helplessness and simplicity of my supplication when I spoke the words. I mention this humiliating detail only because artistic integrity prompts me to.

It is truly strange what kinds of fantasy play out by themselves in my head.

Anyway, after having lived in the country twice, and, besides that, visited at least four times, I have grown familiar with numerous details of Japanese life that were never previously presented to me as characteristic. Of geisha, I have heard (before my first sojourn and since) more times than I can count, and I have even seen geisha, fleetingly, on Pontochô and Gion two or three times. Of space heaters, as a fixture of Japanese life, I heard and knew nothing until at last I was delivered from the Japan of dream to the Japan of experience.

Anyone who has spent much time in Japan will know what I mean. I use the rather odd term 'space heater' because I believe that is the most general equivalent in English and therefore the term with the highest chance of being correct. 'Space heater' has always made me think of something that NASA might send into orbit for the benefit of freezing astronauts, but the object I have in mind, so characteristic of daily life in Japan, is a rather dumpy portable device, usually of the box-like shape that for me suggests the word 'unit', used in an earthbound manner for heating rooms. I believe the designation in Japanese is 'sekiyu sutōbu' (石油ストーブ), which is literally 'oil stove', but might be more accurately rendered as 'paraffin heater'. Certainly, they run on some kind of oil. I remember, during the period of my stay with a family in Kyôto, that early on a cold winter morning, or else at dusk, I would hear the sound of the sekiyu delivery van. Its arrival in the alley was always accompanied by a jingle of some kind, as ice cream vans are in Britain. I always derived a sense of pleasing melancholy from this jingle on a chill winter day. I never saw the van, but I pictured—did I hear?—children skipping rope nearby (really more a British pastime, I think, and even then, a pastime largely of times past), or otherwise playing. I looked up to the dull frosted glass of the window in my room and paid a dreamy kind of attention, as if this sound were something old and friendly and a little bit magical. It was especially evocative to me, for some reason, that this sweet, nursery-rhyme jingle should be associated with something that smelt greasy and foul and that would also bring warmth in the cold, dark nights.

I have, myself, owned and used a sekiyu sutōbu more than once. I especially remember the stove (I will call it such) that I had in my small, ground-floor flat in Kyôto, not far from the Imperial Palace. The problem with the stove—with all such stoves as far as I know—was this: it would heat an enclosed space well enough, but when you turned it off, as you sometimes must, it would give off terrible, at times eye-watering, fumes, and you would have to open a window. Thus, on a winter day, you would swiftly lose all the heat you had gone to such trouble and expense to accumulate.

I had a real sense, using this piece of equipment, that in one way or another it might be the cause of premature death.

I am not convinced, either, that when it was on and the windows were closed, the heat it gave was sufficient to oust the deep Kyôto chill from its winter-long residence in my bones.

In any case, of all the options available to me it was the best, and its idiosyncrasies became part of the texture of my days. When one is lonely and money is limited, I have found, it becomes especially necessary to romanticise such details, as it were, to make friends with every dim and cobwebbed corner of one's life. In other words, there has seldom been a time when I have been able to extract sufficient meaning from my continued existence without such measures. I toss these meagre bones again and again into the soup of life's meaning for stock.

There were three times in particular during the trip around Japan with Bee-chan when I realised consciously what the effect of such conditioning, and the investments I had made in Japan of time, study and emotion, had been. One of these was on our day trip to the hot spring resort, Kusatsu, with Mrs Kurita. We were walking away from the town centre up a long path by a stream leading to one of the famous rotemburo, or open-air baths, though we were not going to bathe there. I had been along this path many years before, when Mr Kurita was alive. That's another story, but I mention it here simply to convey that the route we trod held memories for me.

I suppose it was not the popular season — I remembered the route being busier with foot traffic, and there being more shops and stalls at the side of the path. For a while I even wondered if it was the same path. At a certain point, Mrs Kurita indicated a little box of a shop, detached from other premises, with sliding lattice doors, and suggested we stop here to eat. It was a noodle place—cheap and friendly food, as it seemed to me. I recall this being a welcome halt, probably because I was a little tired and hungry, or else maybe because it was pleasant to stop at a little place by the river like this. Apart from ourselves, there was almost no one there, and it was not one of those places—almost ubiquitous now in the first world—that pipes music to cover the interstitial emptiness that humans increasingly shun and fear. Therefore, when we sat at the central table, we were in the middle of a box full of the quiet of afternoon—the kind of quiet never captured on film. The waiter brought us menus. I ordered tsukimi soba, Bee-chan ordered tempura soba, and what Mrs Kurita ordered might now be lost beyond all hope of recollection.

I remember that the heater was on behind me, and I was hot. I was aware of the oppressive stuffiness of the room. On the one hand, this was simply uncomfortable, but on the other I vaguely enjoyed it, the way you might enjoy the stifling atmosphere of a grandparent's house. I was also aware of the heater itself—a portable, seemingly makeshift means of heating an environment. The sense of its familiarity lingered somewhere at the threshold of my consciousness. It was, despite its mass production, a folk item, like a pair of old leather boots, a twiggy broom or a chicken coop.

Mrs Kurita asked me if I remembered coming here before. I said I did.

"It was this exact shop," she said.

"Was it?" I was doubtful and looked around.

I had a sense that she was right. I recognised the place now, but the recognition was still slightly fuzzy so that I ultimately decided to trust Mrs Kurita's word and I told her that I did, indeed, remember.

Had it been the staff of this shop who had looked after Mr Kurita when he had collapsed on the path outside? As I said, that's another story, but naturally I thought about that time, which apparently shared a place with but was nonetheless unreachably separated from this.

It was good to be here, though I do not wish to exaggerate what I felt. Death and disappearance mark the passage of time somewhat like night falling across the surface of the revolving globe. The difference is that, to our knowledge, what the night of death falls upon does not see day again. So Mr Kurita was now in the remembered dark side of the globe, but we and this shop were still in the daylight of life. When I reflect on it, it seems to me that most pleasures in life are underwritten by a feeling of safety, of which this daylight could be seen as emblematic. Or am I only speaking for myself here? In any case, is it not mysterious that the daylight should bring any sense of safety at all when we know for sure the night is coming, and when all that comes after the night is unknown?

We ate our noodles without much conversation. Mine were unsatisfactory, and I learnt afterwards that I was not alone in this experience. I thought that the raw egg was not as fresh as it should be, perhaps, or that the stock of the soup tasted flat. I had the sense that I might experience some slight digestive turbulence.

While I was contemplating the disappointing noodles, Mrs Kurita hailed the waiter and put it to him that the room was too hot. A little surprised, it seems, he nonetheless acted quickly on her implied request and turned off the oil heater. This is never a quiet affair. The heater gave a great mechanical clank as its flame was extinguished, and then, in strange harmony with my not-quite-right noodles, it sent out invisible billowing waves of paraffin fumes upon the air. At that moment I was overcome with the exquisite consciousness that, indeed, I was in Japan.

Tempted though I am to detail the other two occasions, I see that the above will suffice to make my originally intended point. The reader may refer to the poems in this volume for the remainder. I am consoled by the idea—true or false—that it is always best to keep a little back. The truth is, I am tired. Let us dream of what I did not write, you and I; it will always be so much better than what I did.

Golden Hours Slip By

Sometimes, when I have finished reading a book, I look at my bookshelves and the piles of books upon my floor, and try to decide which I shall read next. Often, as I am doing so, I will see a number of books I had urgently desired to read a long time ago, and which I had determined I would read soon but had subsequently forgotten as I strayed haphazardly in my reading from one urgent timelessness—since books are an attempt to defeat time—to another. I have been reading long enough now to have made some rough calculations about how many books I can read in a lifetime, and I am as certain as I can be that I will never read all the books towards which I have felt this urgent desire. So, at such times, confronted very much with an agony of choice, I often sink into despair. Then I ask myself, again, why I am reading in the first place. Is it to despair, like this, at lack of time?

There was some tension between Bee-chan and me while we were in Japan because she especially wanted to take advantage of the opportunity to lie in of a morning and I especially wanted to take advantage of our geographical position and rise early in order to see more of the temples, museums and other attractions that in Japan so often seem to close at the punitively early hour of four o'clock.

On the ninth of November, in Nagano, Bee-chan had another lie-in. In fact, so did I, though to a lesser extent. We had been considering whether to go to the Jigokudani onsen resort, nearby, famed for its monkeys, who often come down from the mountain slopes and join the outdoor bathers, attracted by the warmth of the water. However, that would have required an early start, a bus journey into the countryside, a hike and so on. It did not happen. Bee-chan lay in the futon after I found myself irrevocably awake, and so I occupied myself in one way or another with indoor morning things, taking less trouble to be quiet as time went on.

Eventually, of course, she rose, and we breakfasted together at about noon. It was a very good breakfast, and I am quite ready to say, one of the best in my life. I have described it elsewhere, so here I shall only say that I was put in mind of Robert Aickman's novel, *The Late Breakfasters*. I thought to myself that it was, indeed, a very good title, and I told myself, too, that I must certainly read it one day, when I get the time.

When we left the ryokan, the day was dull and cold. None of the places we had hoped to go to—such as the Taiwanese tea shop—were open. In fact, Nagano seemed a little dead, as if we had come off season. Since we were just a little too late for the autumn colours and considerably too early for the monkeys—even if we'd gone to the monkey onsen—I suppose, in fact, we had. Anyway, there was no hurry. No one was expecting us, and we were quite free to spend the day, in this town where no one knew us, just as we wished, though what we could effectively wish was limited by what was available.

We turned onto the street that led, in one direction, to Zenkôji, and in the other eventually to the railway station. We took the latter direction. A little way down there was a gap between buildings that gave access to the grounds of a temple. I stopped to look, as such things catch my eye, and was intrigued by a message on a noticeboard in front of the temple building. At the side of the board was written, "This month's message," (今月の言葉) and the message itself read as follows:

> This today that you pass wastefully is the tomorrow that someone who died yesterday desperately wanted to live.
>
> あなたが無駄に過ごした今日は昨日死ん
> だ人がどうしても生きたかった明日
> である。

I took a photograph of it simply as a record of the words.

We continued on our way. I translated the message for Bee-chan and we talked a little about it.

No doubt a worthy sentiment and something we'd do well to recall sometimes, but . . . Agreeing with the message at first, I quickly became suspicious of it.

It was drizzling. Slender trees at the edges of the pavement still had some red leaves—we had not been entirely cheated. I put up the umbrella for us. Even on the street, sentimental music was being quietly piped from somewhere.

In that rainy, off-season resort, a strange warmth began to well up in me. There was really nowhere else I wanted to be and no one else I wanted to be with.

I thought of some words that I find are attributed to J.M. Barrie:

"You must have been warned against letting the golden hours slip by. Yes, but some are golden only because we let them slip."

A Tale of Two Umbrellas

As the reader will know, we acquired, by chance, in Ôsaka, a large, tartan umbrella, quite ample for two. Although the rain was very gentle, it seemed impolite to refuse this gesture from the restaurant staff, and I, for one, was pleased with its picturesqueness. There remained the question, however, of what to do with the umbrella once we returned to our hotel room. An umbrella can be troublesome extra luggage if one is travelling here and there by bus, train and so on, especially when it's dripping. Then again, it might well be needed, and to buy and discard umbrellas whenever it rains is wasteful. But perhaps what really swayed me in favour of keeping the umbrella was the thought of the Japanese word—noun, or adverb?— 'aiaigasa' (相合い傘), which indicates that two people are sharing an umbrella, and which has romantic connotations. We shall be journeying throughout Japan, I thought, under one umbrella (aiaigasa). And so, through that word, this serendipitous umbrella had come to symbolise for me our shared journey.

Yet, after all, what I had decided consciously, fate decided against through the agency of my forgetfulness. When we alighted at Obusé station on the tenth of the month, I left the umbrella behind on the Snow Monkey Express, perhaps hanging from the hook by the window for coats, hats and so on. When I realised this, I felt a sense of helpless distress, such as a child feels when losing a favourite lucky charm. On such occasions, however, we adjust to the new state of being bereft, as we have to, knowing we are born naked, and even our lives are borrowed from our mothers, who borrowed theirs in turn and will return them. I had lost the symbol of our shared journey, but we still had the journey itself, out of which new symbols might be conjured.

I was prompted, also, to reflect on the fate of umbrellas, especially here in Japan: to pass from hand to hand, and more often through chance—by being lost by one person and found by another—than intention. What, then, is the life of an umbrella? What is it to be a disposable shield against foul weather and passive object of fate? If it could, what patchwork tale would an old umbrella tell—what sad picaresque?—of one chance interlude after another? It seems to me it would be a tale very Japanese in spirit, and I would be pleased if some day I could write it. (I have gestured towards it in writing already once or twice.)

The circumstances by which it came to us made the tartan umbrella irreplaceable to me, so that I did not try to replace it. However, necessity intervened. In Kamakura, as we walked to or from Enoshima Beach—which was it?—on an overcast day, it started to rain heavily enough that action of some kind was necessary. We stopped at a convenience store and picked up one of the see-through plastic umbrellas ubiquitous in Japan. I seem to remember us walking down the same road in the evening and discussing what it is like to grow old and die alone, though whether we were under the umbrella at that time or not I don't know.

In fact, that transparent umbrella becomes almost invisible in my memory. Bee-chan stands under it—or one like it—in a photograph taken, I believe, on the edge of neon-garish Kabuki-chô, where she is about to part company with me to do some shopping while I wait in Café de Bore and write. Or, wait, am I holding it as I pose by the illuminated shop sign in a photo taken outside Café de Bore? It is quite possible that it is the same umbrella in both photos—why shouldn't it be? It's just that, thinking of the latter, I seem to remember the dripping umbrella's handle, like a one-pronged grappling hook, at the corner of my small table, where it hung awkwardly in the expensive, pretentious and mediocre café.

Well, it's hardly a great mystery. I only mean to say that, considering how wet much of our remaining time was, memories of the umbrella are elusive. And yet I did not lose this one. I managed to retain it, despite getting very drunk on more than one occasion, right up to our arrival at Narita Airport. There, as we approached security, we saw many signs showing items that were not allowed in hand luggage, and there were bins along the way where you could dispose of such items. None of the signs, as I recall, mentioned umbrellas. I felt something of a dilemma, and I wavered. Should I take it, or leave it? In the end, I felt somehow persuaded to leave it. I looped its handle over one of the security barriers and abandoned it there. I have no idea what became of it, of course. Do umbrellas left at airports get recycled? At this convergence of so many personal journeys, which thus becomes placeless and impersonal as too many footprints obliterate individual tracks, perhaps no one claimed it for a new life and its journey ended with it fading into its own transparency.

But since such an ending will not satisfy some of my readers, I will avail myself of a device I find at the ends of many of the stories collected by the Chinese author Pu Songling.

The Chronicler of the Tales comments: "I had intended to write of two people taking one journey under one umbrella. Instead, I realised that not only were there two umbrellas, there were many journeys, together and apart. The patchwork thus formed is intricate and delicate. We pass from umbrella to umbrella as they pass from person to person. Perhaps human life is as piecemeal as that of the umbrella. That is going too far, no doubt—an umbrella, as far as we know, has no volition. Yet often enough fate treats us as lightly as it does an umbrella. If we can feel sentimental for this peculiar, rain-steeped object, is it not because we know that we may easily be forgotten on a train whose destination is beyond our power to decide? I, and—I do not doubt—you, have experienced something of the kind many times by now. The anguish might be great, or we might only sigh, but try to tell the tale and once more it becomes just another trifling tale of an umbrella."

Pickles/End Titles

I am beginning this section of the book after our return to England and before the jet-lag has worn off. Turkish Airlines, run by a people accustomed to heat, had the air conditioning in their planes at an uncomfortably high temperature, so that I looked forward to cooler English weather. But now, in my poorly heated flat, my fingers are stiff with cold. England is often depicted as a land of mediocrity, but the cold and the early dark strike me today as somewhat severe and it's hard for me to resist the impression that this cold and darkness says something about my future prospects. It is my task in this book, however, to look back, not forward, or at least that is how I intend to write this final section.

It is Tuesday today. We arrived back at Heathrow some time after nine o'clock on Saturday night, the 21st of November, 2015. We wondered what the exact difference in temperature might be between Japan and England, and, as if on cue, someone who had apparently travelled the same route, also changing at Istanbul, said to her travelling companions, "London is twelve degrees colder than Japan."

On the Piccadilly Line, I observed to Bee-chan that the trains here were narrower (their passengers, on average, larger), so that people facing each other on London trains are in danger of touching toes, which they certainly are not in Tôkyô. I parted from Bee-chan at Piccadilly Circus, to change again at Charing Cross for Bexleyheath.

I was reassured to find my flat intact, though various things were making a cabbagey stench in the fridge, and, despite a neighbour looking in during my absence, more of my plants had withered.

It was a relief, after the long and uncomfortable journey, with almost no sleep, to get into my own bed, but I shivered under the duvet and was depressed to notice the damp smell of the room and the bed itself—like that of an abandoned house. I wondered if I would ever, in my life, escape the rawness and insecurity that the cold air and the damp smell expressed to me now with such intimate immediacy.

Exhaustion, anyway, promised me sleep, though it was not as swift as I might have expected. I felt the tide of sleep begin to rise around me, and was aware that it contained the particular melancholy that heavy exhaustion sometimes brings, along with the tingling fatalism that is another of exhaustion's common accompaniments.

And in the midst of this, images from the newly concluded trip rose up in my mind with the haunting freshness of the recent past—so close as to be almost as present to the senses as the current moment in time, but just far enough, now, also, to be unmistakably beyond recovery, to have shifted from the joyous immediacy of life to the vaguely sinister, phantasmal world of memory. Lying there in that cold, faintly damp bed, exhausted and on the verge of sleep, was one of those occasions in life when the very fact of the present forever becoming past is a heartache for which there is no consolation. On such occasions, you feel so naked and so helpless before fate—which is to say, the rolling cosmos in which you are embedded—that the feeling itself is a kind of death, not without a tinge of relief at letting go, as if, realising no fight of yours can save you now, you lie back in a thrill of distress and allow yourself to be strangled.

When death is near enough that it seems certain, your life is said to pass before your eyes. 'Flash' is the word customarily used, but I would prefer to use something else—'parade', perhaps. Your life is said to parade before you, albeit at a faster than walking pace. I am not aware of a specific instance of this rumour being substantiated (for all I know, there are millions), but it appeals to me at some instinctive level. Life can be lived again in a split second, and the split seconds of this second life can be, we must assume, similarly expanded. Perhaps it is not even the same life repeated. Ambrose Bierce used this idea in his 'An Occurrence at Owl Creek Bridge', since when it has been used as a supposedly original twist in countless books and films.

The images that came back to me as I lay in bed were not exactly of this type, but I would like to compare them. There is often a suggestion of mixed exhilaration and reassurance in the mention of the parade of memories at life's end, and if there is sadness, it is the sadness of fireworks, of the culmination of something, and there is an insoluble ambiguity as to whether the grand finale implies an afterlife or whether it implies none. But the sadness in these images of the recent past consisted in the fact that life itself was not at an end—these good things had passed, but I lived on. In that sense, the feeling was more closely comparable to grief, to the uprush of memories and the realisation of loss that occurs when *someone else* dies. A similar emotion is known to people beyond number from the experience of a love affair ending.

So, like a tragic hero of myth, I looked back when I had been forbidden to, and saw love and beauty in the pale face of the memory I had been leading out from the underworld and knew that in my desire for this beautiful spectre I lost her to the underworld forever—forever, and, no doubt, a day—and nothing could be done (at least not until the underworld opened its portals and received petitions once more).

The images had a fleetingness independent of time and most of them disappeared before I could identify or grasp them. One image—really a short sequence of time, containing sound and smell, too—remained. For some reason, my mind fixed finally on that one image as if it contained the essence of all the others. I will describe the image—or sequence—itself in a short while, but I am afraid it will be meaningless to the reader without some background, which I shall provide first. For me, of course, all the background I can describe and more was already present in the sequence—or image—itself.

I suppose it started in a stand-up bar, but the bar was in Sendai, and we might not have found it if we had not been looking for a ryokan in the area because of dissatisfaction with the ryokan where we had booked a room and were staying. With apologies to those whose native sentiments belong to Sendai, I have to say, we were disappointed in the city from our arrival. Well, no doubt the city had not asked us to come, and it was perhaps naïve to expect it to be very different to other large Japanese cities, with their interchangeable cereal-packet skyscrapers. However, the small town of Obusé aside, this was the first place in Japan that we had planned to visit that neither of us had been to before, we had some vague idea that the north might be more rustic than average, and there was at least some sense of anticipation in the thought of exploring new territory. The concept of travel itself, however, was almost rendered meaningless by the cityscape that confronted us when we left Sendai Station. Why not just spend more time in Ôsaka or Tôkyô? People are apt to mention the film *Blade Runner* in an attempt to describe Japanese cities, but there is a majestic, baroque quality to the megalopolis scenes of *Blade Runner* and, thinking back on Sendai, I am more inclined to compare it to some of the sets of the original Star Trek. Imagine a planet that was not to receive much air-time in the show, but for which, design-wise, a simple, visual shorthand was needed to convey a highly urbanised society. With little time and money, the set designers might have concocted a city of straight lines and metal surfaces like those seen on the outside of armoured vehicles, with long slits where square blocks of light appeared, marking windows—a city otherwise featureless and culture-less, and impressive largely in the sheer cliff-face of its sterility, on which life might not be expected to find any finger-hold at all. Perhaps a tangle of bridges or

133

walkways between buildings would suffice to give the impression of labyrinthine bewilderment such a city would need for the purposes of the show.

Such was my first impression of Sendai.

In relation to Japan I have often felt an unquenchable grief because the relentless urbanisation seems an obliteration of the past rather than an outgrowth of it, but I must not exaggerate, here, the disappointment I experienced on account of Sendai providing one more example of this depressing phenomenon. I reminded myself that place is inseparable from time, and because time, while it exists at all, does not stop, each moment is unique, and this uniqueness, therefore, is also bestowed upon the drabbest and most undistinguished of places. On the whole, I was satisfied with this and looking forward to exploring our unique time in Sendai even if Sendai itself was not prepossessing.

The mood slumped distinctly into gloom, however, when we arrived at our lodgings, Morishigé Ryokan. We were shown along twists and turns of corridor, hollow-sounding beneath our feet, to Room 101. On a crimson square in the entry hall was a mat of dark brown, varnished bamboo shoots on which to place one's slippers. The interior had dark blue wallpaper that looked as if it were patterned on an old serge haori. The floor was tatami-matted and an embroidered piece of fabric covered the adjustable, wood-framed mirror. This last detail emphasised to me what this place had in common with the lodgings we had just left, in Nagano. But this resemblance also served to make the differences more noticeable. The Nagano room had had the brisk freshness often associated with what is popularly called a Japanese minimalist aesthetic. Our current room was stale, as if there had been little circulation of air to renew the place in decades. In fact, one might imagine it was the lack of a fresh breeze that preserved the décor in its rather dated style. I should be clear: I liked the dated décor, and I liked the shabbiness, though had received enough of a dent in my impressions on this account that I soon fell in with Bee-chan's mood of despondency when she expressed it.

When the proprietress had left us to settle in, Bee-chan first said that the room looked like a survival from the eighties. I am no expert, but to me, the décor seemed older—vintage, you might say. True, it was a little kitsch, but in a way that might excite someone specialising in recreating period interiors for films. I would have placed the overall feel as early sixties. In any case, it evoked for me, strongly, that distinct period of modern Japanese history after World War II and before the Bubble of the eighties. I could imagine a sixties screen idol or star of enka—Watari Tetsuya, for instance—being photographed in such a setting for the jacket of a single.

For me, in fact, this had, at first, made up to some extent for my disappointment with the city itself, but for Bee-chan it had drastically worsened that disappointment. I had recognised in that little room a validation of my redemptive feeling that each moment is unique. Another, different time had been preserved for us to demonstrate this, even if that preservation had necessarily involved the dusty staleness that is, for time, the equivalent of perspective in spatial distance. For the sake of depth in the present, not everything, anyway, can be new. We need a biodiversity of the temporal if culture is not to stagnate, and this room was like an underground cave where a precious ecosystem had survived in isolation. It recorded for us the styles and fashions, the consistent underlying atmosphere, of another era. For this reason, I read in these surroundings signs of life in a way that I had not in the environs of Sendai Station.

The name of the ryokan was Morishigé—probably a family name. Read literally, however, 'mori' is 'forest' and 'shigé' is 'luxuriant growth'—'verdant forest' or 'overgrown forest' depending on one's point of view. That is, in the former case, it is a place of life, in the latter case, a place of neglect. This might describe the differing views that Bee-chan and I had of our lodgings. In either case, it is true that, beneath the forest canopy, the prevailing atmosphere is a kind of gloom.

After commenting on the décor, Bee-chan took a torch—electric—from its wall bracket, examined it, and passed it to me.

"Can you see how to turn this on?" she asked.

The torch had a slot-like hole near one end, but other than that seemed featureless. I could find no on-off switch.

"No, I can't," I said.

"I think it's meant to turn on automatically when you take it from the wall."

I agreed. The slot was no doubt central to the mechanism.

Bee-chan replaced the torch in its bracket. There had been something tense and purposeful in her questions about the torch, but I did not understand it until a while later, when she said she was not happy in this place and she thought we should find somewhere else. If they hadn't bothered to check on the torch, she asked, what else might they have neglected to check on? Clearly, the torch itself was not the issue, but had been identified as a telling detail. I became attuned, myself, to Bee-chan's mood, at least inasmuch as I was now seeing our room in Morishigé Ryokan as somewhere we had unfortunately 'ended up' because we were ill-informed on local conditions.

I smoked a cigarette in the verandah area, which existed between two sets of sliding doors, the second set overlooking the urban scenery outside. I sat on a thin floor-cushion and tapped my ash into the ashtray that had been on the low table in the adjoining space. I felt heavy, but also light. I was anxious, but felt detached from my anxiety. This thin cushion in this narrow verandah space seemed to represent a tiny island of time. The floor held my weight, though the moment that held the floor would melt like a snowflake. We were here temporarily to begin with, but it seemed likely we would leave before the end of our reservation. Somehow the temporariness of the situation — this time, and contrary to my usual experience — made me feel safe. Everything, of course, would pass, but this moment held me up as if the cushion were a hovering magic carpet — a seedy magic carpet, to be sure, on which I smoked a cigarette and looked out at the grimy view of canyoned streets.

I phoned another ryokan that Bee-chan had mentioned. We could not visit them tonight, but we could have a look in the morning. However, now that it was settled that we would look for another place, the mood had lightened a little, and we decided we should go out for a drink. Since the ryokan we had phoned was in walking distance, we were also inclined to see if we could find it, and take a peek from outside, while we were looking for places to drink. The area didn't have a great deal to interest foot-passengers, but the cool night air was refreshing—the cold of which we had been warned had no sting. We made a turning we remembered or deduced from a preparatory comparison of maps. About halfway down this street, on our left, since the road was on our right, we saw something that immediately caught our attention as a humorous novelty. It was a standing bar, perhaps slightly larger than the wardrobe on one side of the hallway of my small flat. From about waist height it was a brightly lit kiosk of glass in which were visible a counter, a person behind the counter, and the suited backs of perhaps four men in front of the counter—three on its long side, one on its short side. For some reason, being indoors seems to allow humans a particular atmosphere of intimacy that does not occur in the open air. It was slightly peculiar to see that intimacy through this glass. It wasn't even the glass—it was that the area the glass enclosed was so small.

"We could go in there," I joked.

But why was this a joke?

Bee-chan questioned me, obviously not sure that I was serious. I hadn't been, but I suddenly wondered why not. Of course, we might not have been able to squeeze in, anyway, but this was not—I think—what had made my suggestion a joke. There was something intimidating about a bar of such cramped proportions—it was the intimidation that provoked the humour. First of all, there was the suspicion that those who entered such a bar must, in some way, know what they are doing, perhaps because they know each other. They would, one suspected, be regulars from time immemorial. Then there was the point-blank proximity of the counter which, even aside from the elbow-to-elbow presence of other customers, meant confronting whoever was serving you nose-to-nose the whole time you were there. As far as conversation was concerned, this was not tennis—it was ping pong.

Yet something about the little bar had snagged me. In youth we become tormented by the idea that each failure to dare to do something is a death that marks, in the branching pathways of eternity, one more turn away from the pure, sweet life that is the only life worthy of the name. Some of us grow dull to such thoughts. I felt a partial revival of them at the suggestion in my exchange with Bee-chan that it would be preposterous to enter the bar. Anyway, we did not stop, but even as we talked, passed by. Maybe we would come back, but first we would see if we could locate the ryokan. Even if the doors were closed and there was nothing to be seen, our task would be easier in the morning.

We came to a junction and turned left, walking now along a road that, though still wide, seemed clearly at one remove from the main road, and had, therefore, a backstreet feel. Here, we peered at two or three places to eat, but were not especially tempted by any of them. Forgetting the advice we'd received on the phone, that the ryokan was tucked away in an alley, we failed, also, to locate this supposedly secondary object of our search. Thinking we must have passed it without realising, we turned back. We still had not found it when we were once more in the vicinity of the stand-up bar. This time there appeared to be only two occupants—

the person behind the bar and a single customer, or perhaps another member of staff, in front of the bar. This second figure appeared to belong so decidedly to the bar, it was hard to tell whether she worked there or not.

We stopped—I am not sure why. We were tired, and perhaps we saw a chance to redeem ourselves for not entering the bar earlier. We wondered if they served food—it seemed unlikely—and looked outside for the bill of fare. Those inside could not help noticing us, the intimacy of their little space being as permeable as it was to the outside world. The second figure first gestured to the figure behind the bar, then both of them began to gesture to us. They had about them the animation of anglers not wanting to lose a catch. In any case, it was clear we did not need introductions, and whatever reservations we might have had, it now seemed the natural and pleasing thing to do to enter, and so we did.

We had to sidle in, the space being so narrow. I stood at the short side of the counter and Bee-chan stood at a right angle to me. From this point on my memory becomes progressively more unreliable. In the inside pocket of my jacket I have a business card that one of the young women in the bar gave me. Looking at it now, I see that, on the left, it has a cartoon character pulling at the edges of his mouth with his fingers and blowing a raspberry. Next to this is written, "Berobero Bar". Consulting my dictionary, I find 'berobero' to be an adverb indicating a degree of drunkenness—a high degree. Perhaps it is onomatopoeia for the rolling of a tongue around the mouth in the slurred speech of the inebriated subject. It explains, anyway, the cartoon figure. During our relatively short time in the bar, (I cannot speak for Bee-chan, but) I made considerable advances on the road towards the attainment of the condition depicted.

Things became hazy. Alcohol is a curious substance. It can be used to remove things, as with rubbing alcohol, but also to keep things, as when they are preserved in alcohol. The drinks we were served at that bar have done a mixture of the two things to my memory of the bar. But then, I believe we mixed our drinks.

The alcohol has wiped much away, but what remains is as if highlighted, wreathed as it is by the particular mist that makes the drunkard wish to sing misty songs. I shall try, therefore, to capture with a drunken—even with a *berobero*—pen, those details that loom, in my memory, out of the erasing and preserving mist.

The two young women who welcomed us at some point gave their ages, which I recall as late twenties and early thirties, though both could easily have passed for being in their early twenties, and one of them—the one behind the bar—might have been asked for I.D. in a pub in the U.K. They also told us their names, which I attempted to remember and subsequently forgot. Of course, I do have that business card I mentioned, which gives at least one of their names, which I shan't reproduce here. I say "at least one of their names" because there's something odd about the card. There is another name on it, which I remember now as the name given by the young woman in front of the bar. However, on the card, it appears to be the name of the establishment itself. Was she the boss? Of course, this is possible, but a single detail makes me doubt it. This name is the name also of the street block on which the bar was located. I think I shall have to leave this mystery unsolved.

Whether their relationship was primarily personal or professional, the two seemed to know each other well. I shall call the young woman behind the counter, Ai, and the young woman leaning on the counter, Yuina. Ai had a typically cute Japanese look, with a straight fringe across her forehead, long straight hair, and bright, liquid eyes emphasised by mascara. Yuina, a little taller, had a slightly more tomboyish demeanour. She wore a gauze mask, as the Japanese often do when they have a cold in order to protect others from their germs, but she had pulled this down so that it covered her chin rather than her mouth and nose. She was clearly tired of trying to talk through her mask. The lowered mask, therefore, looked a little like the kerchief of a cowboy in a western—an impression reinforced by her posture, which was somewhat of the kind that might make you expect her to say, "Set 'em up, barman!"

Ai prepared little bowls for us of something that she said was on the house. Such generosity is so common in Japan that one might begin to take it for granted, but presumably this came out of her wages, or necessitated a similar arrangement. I don't remember exactly what the bowls contained. (I don't have a great memory for food, anyway.) It might have been something like prawn salad. At any rate, it tasted good and was appreciated, but was, I believe, all we ate at that bar.

As I recall, we started on lager and moved quickly on to spirits, whether vodka, whisky or something else, I am no longer sure. Ai and Yuina asked us questions, among the first of which was whether we liked alcohol (they were gratified to learn that we did). The conversation did not exactly flow, but our two hosts were diligent. They audibly and visibly thought up new questions, apparently unabashed to make such deliberate conversation, and because they were unabashed, even this deliberate conversation did not seem particularly awkward. There were lulls, it was true, while Ai and Yuina concocted their next questions, and it was apparent during these lulls that two of us were strangers to the other two and that one pair might have little in common with the other. This was not entirely comfortable, but goodwill is like a global language that has no literature. Its existence around the world might easily be overlooked, but when noticed strikes one as a remarkable phenomenon worth studying. The slight sense of atmospheric discomfort also began to melt for me as the alcohol entered my bloodstream. I began to lose the tense, alert and generalised sense of responsibility that, though necessary to social beings, would perhaps cause insanity if it were entirely inescapable, and which certainly is incompatible—for instance—with great or serious art.

Somehow, at quite an early stage in the conversation, the subject of music came up. Bee-chan showed Yuina something on her iPod, and it was apparent they both liked the same obscure Japanese band (I have since been reminded it was Maximum the Hormone). I think this is something that Bee-chan had in common with Yuina that Ai didn't. Nor did I, for that matter. Although this topic of conversation didn't lead anywhere, it nonetheless helped kindle the sense of occasion and create an expectation that there might be other things to talk about, even if those things were only a kind of pleasant game of pot luck played by two pairs of humans who would normally be separated by thousands of miles and that great gulf of obscurity in which every life—unbeknown to itself—generally exists, from the point of view of the world at large, or of most other individuals in that world.

An imagined language barrier was a source of something like amusement to me. With a few minor tweaks, a skilful scriptwriter could have made the conversation actually quite funny. Naturally, Ai and Yuina expected us to have little or no Japanese, and, when we first entered, attempted to speak English to us. I tend to feel it's a little pushy to answer in Japanese when one is spoken to in English. Even so, it was clear that my Japanese, whatever its faults might be, would be more conducive to a meaningful conversation than their English, or, at least, that a conversation conducted entirely in English would be limited and frustrating. However, even when I began to speak in Japanese and they answered me in Japanese, it seemed not to have registered that we had switched from English to Japanese, and that English could be dispensed with. If they had simply wished to practise their English, that would have been understandable, but both appeared to labour under the impression that they had to dredge up all the English phrases they could remember in order to be understood. This culminated in Ai, with an air of having solved a difficult problem, taking out a gadget of some kind, typing in her question or answer in Japanese, and holding up the screen to us to show us what she presumably thought was a translation supplied by the gadget. Perhaps the device was on the wrong setting. What it actually showed was simply what she had written in Japanese, and, beneath it, the very same thing, but rendered phonetically in the Roman alphabet. This wasn't entirely unhelpful, as it served to confirm or correct what I thought I had heard, but I did wonder whether she noticed, or what she made of the fact that I was responding in her own language to these improvised subtitles.

At one point in the conversation, the question came up—or, as I recall it, returned—of our nationality in relation to our first language. I believe that both the fact we spoke English and the fact we were from England had already been made known in one way or another, but a renewal of one of these questions led to a renewal of the other:

"England? You're from England? Do they speak English in England?"

After asking us directly, Ai conferred with Yuina.

The question does not sound quite as ridiculous in Japanese as in English, since the word for 'English' is 'Eigo' and the word for 'England' is 'Igirisu'. Still, it was slightly bemusing to be asked such a thing. I felt the usual irritation, which arises from associating such ignorance with the cultural prominence of the U.S.A. and with American global hegemony over a language that did not originate in America. But apart from having grown used to such irritation, partly through un-American fatalism, I was also aware of mitigating circumstances in this case. Ai and Yuina were obviously aware of and embarrassed by their ignorance. I felt peculiarly sorry for them, then a little ashamed of myself. It was even pleasant, I decided, to be reminded that you are not the centre of the universe. What need, really, did Ai and Yuina have to know about England here, in this tiny, stand-up bar, or in the lives that were attached to it? I thought of the television series I had seen long ago of *The Hitchhiker's Guide to the Galaxy* (I haven't read the book). I remembered how the series began with the Earth being demolished to make way for an intergalactic hyperway, or some such thing, so that the story itself was built upon the absence of a centre—of what to humans has always been the centre of all things. How a human refugee from a vanished Earth would feel in real life is hard to say, but imaginatively, in the context of the television series, the loss of Earth affected me with a kind of liberating sadness. In this case, anyway, in the bar in Sendai, England was not destroyed, it was simply that its centrality—always questionable at best—had been neatly, and even inadvertently, negated. With the concept of centrality gone, we were released from our cultural orbits, floating in space—hitchhiking. The interesting thing is that such galactic hitchhikers still find something to say to each other, as if they have common ancestry in the void of space itself.

The bar had become a space capsule. G.K. Chesterton, concocting an analogy to convey the preciousness of contingent existence, tells us that each object rescued from a shipwreck on a desert island becomes an ideal object. To adapt that analogy to the one I have developed here, in space, everything is flotsam and jetsam. Imagine the wonder of being adrift in a capsule in space and seeing, floating your way, from some unknown when and where, a teapot, a record player or a book of matches.

While we had been in Kyôto, Bee-chan had been eager to buy some pickles, for which Kyôto is famous, but had put the matter off more than once, as one sometimes does, thinking there will be a later opportunity, and there hadn't been. At some point, Bee-chan's fondness for pickles must have come up in the conversation, and Ai seemed glad of the opportunity to present her with a meaningful gift. She had pickles to hand, and gave Bee-chan a little sealed-plastic package of them, like space-food.

I began to feel more distinctly, in that bar, what I had felt vaguely in our lodgings earlier—a sense that there was some meaning in having travelled to Sendai, after all. It is true, I would have been deeply gratified if our travel had been made meaningful on the scale of the city itself, but it was this plastic packet of pickles, instead, that had restored the meaning of travel for us.

We chatted for a while longer but eventually were given to understand it was time to close up. I think we ordered last drinks, or, no, I remember the downing of drinks not yet near the bottom of the glass. It must have been before this, then, that we asked Ai and Yuina about the hostel we had been looking for. We gave the address, perhaps consulting a map on someone's phone. In any case, we were told it would have been on precisely the street where we had looked and failed to find it.

We were given business cards and invited to come again. At the time, for a few moments perhaps, it seemed to me that we might, but then I knew that we wouldn't and, indeed, we didn't. I knew I had a headache coming on and swallowed some painkillers and, in the euphoria of carelessness that alcohol brings, we turned back in the direction from which we had last come, to have another try at locating the hostel. This time, we found it. It was not facing the street, but, as we had been told and should have remembered, tucked a little way down an alley.

The front door was open, and the genkan and reception were lit, but there was no one around and the place was pleasantly silent—the silence that speaks not of desertion but of sleep.

"What do you think?" I asked, as we peered in.

"Not much different to where we're staying now."

The next morning, we slept in. We didn't keep our appointment with the proprietors of the other hostel. Bee-chan's misgivings about Morishigé Ryokan apparently subsided.

After Sendai, we went on to Kamakura, and from Kamakura to Gunma, staying first in Ôta-shi and then in Maébashi. From Maébashi, we took the local train to Tôkyô, where we stayed for two days with Jbon and two days with friends of Bee-chan.

It is in Tôkyô that this tale concludes. We were aware, I think, of being near the end of our journey. Our rail passes had expired on the day we travelled from Kamakura to Gunma, I was determined to take out no more money and less than a week remained to us. The anxieties of travel are many, as are the causes it can bring for sensations of liberty and expansion. In this case, the slipping-and-sliding freedom of knowing we were reaching the end of something and would pull loose from its gravity was coloured by the fact that our flight from this would be back to what we knew as normal life. Such feelings of anxiety and excitement come back to me when I think of the coin locker in Ikébukuro Station.

Bee-chan's backpack had been a troublesome burden to her throughout the holiday. She proposed, therefore, that we leave all the luggage we would not need for the next couple of days (and perhaps until our return to Britain) in one of the larger coin lockers, allowing us to feel something of the lightness of relief for the final period of our stay. This is what we did, though I was also anxious at leaving things in this metal box in the station.

Once we had taken the receipt from the locker, we walked from the station to Jbon's flat. He'd left the key for us and we let ourselves in, settling for a while after the strains of our journey.

We visited the locker twice after first depositing luggage there. Once was to take out some things we needed before staying with Bee-chan's friends, and once was to empty the locker preparatory to our journey home. It was the second time we opened the locker door—just before going on to stay with Bee-chan's friends—that we were first aware of a strange smell emanating from somewhere, either the locker itself or something in our luggage. It was a stale, pungent, cheesy smell, not unlike that of sweaty socks that have been left unwashed in a laundry basket for a week or so. In fact, I first suspected that an item of unwashed clothing might be the culprit, but after a little searching in bags and sniffing of objects, we were unable to find the exact item or anything else that might be the source. Deciding to attend to the mystery later, we took out what we needed and returned the rest, paying a further fee and receiving a receipt for the opening and closing of the door and the extension of our use of the metal cavity.

It was in our last two or three days that the mystery was solved in a simple but unexpected way. We were in the guestroom of the house where we were staying immediately prior to our return flight and Bee-chan said to me, "By the way, I found the source of the smell when I was repacking."

"Really? What was it?"

"It was those pickles. You know, the ones from Sendai that we got given in that tiny bar. There was a little hole in the packaging and it was leaking."

"Oh no! I suppose it's got over everything now."

"No, it's not too bad. I've separated the pickles and wrapped them up in several layers of plastic bags. I think they should be okay now."

This measure, of course, was taken in order that she might still carry the pickles home. That she went to such lengths could be seen as evidence of her fondness for pickles, her appreciation of the gift, or a consciousness that we would have few, if any, chances to buy such pickles now, or all these things in combination. I thought it was better, too, not to waste the pickles if it was possible to keep them, though it was also a little worrying to have a leaking item in the luggage.

Our holiday was tumbling, falling, to its termination. On our last full day, however, we had some moments of peacefulness and relaxation. Agreeing that the time we had spent at Kamakura had been too brief, we decided to return and walk along one of the hiking routes recommended in the guidebook. After alighting at Kita-Kamakura Station, we stopped on a whim—attracted by the thatched gate at the head of a stairway—at Tôkeiji, which we learnt, reading the literature given to us, was referred to as, "The Divorce Temple". It was a leafy and a mossy place, a series of stairways between foliage, all canopied by tall cryptomeria and other trees. There are very few occasions of genuine calm in life—at least, not in mine. That is, few moments blessed by the forgetfulness of time, that return one to the essential truth—if it is truth, which we must hope and perhaps trust—that what we call now, being the basis of all reality, is the stoniest stone and the rockiest rock there is, that is to say, if now is not a rock, then nothing is, including what we call rock; few moments that, in having returned us to this true rock of now, allow the feeling of sunlight to penetrate its dormancy and moss to grow and spread upon it, an emblem of the only kind of wealth possible to human beings: that of experience, feeling and understanding. Looking upon a statue of a standing Buddha among a grove of tall bamboo canes, the statue and grove seeming to occur naturally together, I felt something of the calm described above. I felt it as a soothing caress, as an emotional delight and as a philosophical insight—in short, as something, though subtle, wonderfully objective.

Is it strange that such peace should abound in the grounds of the Divorce Temple? But what divorce meant in this case was sanctuary. If a woman, abused by her husband, came to the temple and lived here for three years, divorce was granted to her. We must accept that peace sometimes comes from severance rather than union.

After Tôkeiji, a little way down the road, we found a place to have lunch. We sat in the zashiki area and were served ramen by an enthusiastically polite waiter. Then, refreshed, we began our hike in earnest, up the wooded hills overlooking Kamakura, and stopping only once, at the Kuzuharaoka Shrine, a place of dappled sunlight at the time of our visit, which seemed to complement the sober shade of Tôkeiji by its superstitious celebration of romantic love. Here were two rocks tied together by enchanted ropes—a female rock and a male—and unglazed plates to throw at another rock for good luck, and heart-shaped wooden plaques on which to write one's petitions for love. If Tôkeiji had brought me calm, the shrine added a lemony tinge of hope.

And so, as I recall, we continued our hike in good spirits, pausing now only briefly to admire the view, for instance, between susuki plants, across the massed foliage of the hills, to the intricate, clustered zigzags of the roofs and thoroughfares of Kamakura, and out to the sun-sheen and cloud-haze of the sea, beyond.

At the end of the hike we saw together the Daibutsu, or Great Buddha, which on our previous visit I had seen alone. Bee-chan made some sketches here and I, oddly moved by the conjunction of thoughts and feelings I had had during the hike and impressions that came to me with my second viewing of the Great Buddha, wrote a poem that was really little more than a translation, or mistranslation, of a poem on a signboard by a bench in the grounds surrounding the Great Buddha—a poem that coincided with my mood remarkably. I translated the poem as I understood it and added a line. After all, I think I misunderstood it, but the resulting poem captures something of the sense of deep spiritual reassurance I had in those moments.

My memory of our train journey back from Kamakura to Tôkyô is that we spoke little. I was full, as if truly nourished by my recent experience. I had a sense that Bee-chan felt the same, but I do not know. Often such assumptions are mistaken. Anyway, we are nearing the end of this little story—if you will indulge me in calling it a story—and perhaps the reader is even impatient with me. All I have written is—as I explained near the beginning—the background to a single image, that came back to me as I lay awake in my cold, damp bed, after our return to England, a single memory, like a moment replayed in the end titles when a film is over.

I don't think I can pinpoint exactly when the memory belongs to. It might have been after our Kamakura hike, or even the next morning, as we were getting ready to leave for Narita airport and our flight home. Anyway, we were in the bedroom of the house belonging to the friends of Bee-chan and another adjustment of luggage—minor or major, penultimate or final— was taking place. Bee-chan saw that her improvising with layers of plastic bags had not entirely succeeded in its intended effect.

"These pickles are a nightmare," she said.

Later, perhaps on the shuttle bus to the airport, or perhaps at the airport itself, she told me she had thrown the pickles away, after all.

Appendices
語彙と図

Glossary

Bizen-yaki—A kind of pottery produced by the traditional techniques of the historical Bizen Province. Characteristically, it has little or no glaze and a reddish, rustic finish. I really know little about it, despite my love of Japanese ceramics, but citing it by name helps me feel like a connoisseur.

Ema—A wooden plaque, usually decorated and of about postcard size, used for petitionary prayers at Shinto shrines. In my observation, the things most commonly wished for are to pass one's exams and to find love. It is sometimes comforting to think that life might be so simple. Could it be that it is?

Enka—A popular style of song that arose in the post-war era, usually taking the form of sentimental ballads. How I remember Mr Kurita singing a karaoke version of 'Saké Yo!' in a tiny bar in Maébashi.

Genkan—The entry hall in a Japanese home, and specifically the space from which one *steps up* to the floor of the home itself. This is why one traditional welcome to a Japanese home is *"O-agari kudasai"*, or "Please come up."

Gyôza—Often referred to in English as "dumplings"; I tend to think of them more as miniature Chinese pasties.

Haori—A kind of traditional jacket. Literally, I think, 'woven wings'.

Izakaya—A traditional Japanese drinking establishment. It is usual, in such places, to eat while one drinks. Dishes are ordered in the style of tapas, for those at a table to share. Very much preferable to the British pub.

Kawara—The tiles used for the traditional curved roof.

Matcha—Powdered green tea.

Metcha shibui—This is an expression or exclamation of approval. 'Metcha' is a colloquial term meaning 'very'. 'Shibui' is somewhat harder to explain, partly because I am not confident that I understand it. However, it is a word that I find deeply attractive, and I tend to think of it as an adjective describing 'geezer chic'.

Omoshiroi—The Japanese word for 'interesting'. It has, however, what to many English speakers is a confusing ambiguity, as it is also the primary adjective used for 'funny' or 'amusing'.

Onsen—A hot spring, especially as utilised for public bathing.

Sencha—Green tea in its most popular Japanese form.

Shibui—See '*Metcha shibui*' above.

Shôji—A traditional sliding door with paper over latticework.

Sumi-e—An ink-wash painting style using black ink, generally making use of background void to give a suggestion of the infinite.

Susuki—(*Miscanthus sinensis*) Similar to the pampas grass once common in British gardens, this is a perennial plant with wispy ears on long stalks rising above its clumped, ribbon-like leaves. Despite being perennial, it is, in Japan, especially associated with late summer and early autumn. Could this be because of the way the ears catch the rays of a setting sun, or is that merely a fancy of mine?

Tanka—The form of poetry or, literally 'short song', from which haiku developed. Tanka generally have 31 syllables. The pattern is 5-7-5-7-7. The first three lines, of seventeen syllables, are the derivation of haiku. I am not sure how many would acknowledge the poems in the present volume as tanka, and I don't insist they are called such, but certainly I have modelled them on tanka.

Tatami—Floor matting made of rice straw. Traditionally, rooms in Japan are measured by the number of tatami mats.

Tsukemono—Pickles. To a British reader, this immediately brings to mind either pickled onions or pickled gherkins. However, there is a wider variety of pickled goods in Japan. Pickled items include radish, turnip, cucumber, lotus root and aubergine.

Ukigumo—*Floating Clouds.* The title of a novel by the fascinating Hayashi Fumiko.

Ukiyo-e—Literally, pictures of the floating world. The woodblock prints of downtown Edo. Hokusai is perhaps the most famous practitioner of this art.

Yama kuri—Mountain chestnut (*castanea crenata*).

Yukata—A light kimono, often used in the manner of a bathrobe or in hot summer weather.

Washiki—Japanese-style, particularly when referring to a tatami-matted room, without chairs, appointed with traditional Japanese décor.

Map of Voyage

Y